Against
the
Dying
of the
Light

Against *the* Dying *of the* Light

A FATHER'S JOURNEY THROUGH LOSS

L EONARD F EIN

JEWISH LIGHTS PUBLISHING

Woodstock, Vermont

Against the Dying of the Light:
A Father's Journey through Loss

© 2001 Leonard Fein

Library of Congress Cataloging-in-Publication Data
Fein, Leonard J.
Against the dying of the light : a father's journey through loss / Leonard Fein.
       p.   cm.
ISBN 1-58023-110-1 (hc)
1. Fein, Leonard J.   2. Fein, Nomi, d. 1996.   3. Jews—
United States—Biography.   4. Bereavement.   5. Consolation.
I. Title.
E184.37.F44 A3   2001
296.7—dc21   00-012801

Manufactured in the United States of America
Cover design by Drena Fagen
Text design by Susan Ramundo

For People of All Faiths, All Backgrounds
Published by Jewish Lights Publishing
A Division of LongHill Partners, Inc.
Sunset Farm Offices, Route 4, P.O. Box 237
Woodstock, VT 05091
Tel: (802) 457-4000   Fax: (802) 457-4004
www.jewishlights.com

Rage, rage against the dying of the light.

—Dylan Thomas,
"Do not go gentle into that good night"

Contents

Foreword

BACK THEN, IT WAS CATHARTIC. THE WRITING BEGAN JUST DAYS after she died, and I understood from the start that the act of writing was a way both to keep her alive and to accept the fact of her death. And I needed to do both.

Much time has passed since then, and new purposes have unfolded. Somewhat to my surprise, what I'd supposed was an attempt to set down the details of Nomi's life and death, at the least as a legacy for her daughter, became something more, became an account of my own experience with my daughter's death.

Even now, several years later, the very act of writing the words "my daughter's death," of seeing those words on the computer screen, is startling. It is a hammer blow. But whatever temptation there is to use a gentler term, no evasion alters the fact. Therein rests the singular significance of death: It is unalterable. It is a verdict that cannot be appealed. The computer on which I compose these words pulls in precisely the opposite direction: It invites revision, encourages editing. Most often, our lives, like the computer on which I write, offer ongoing reassurance: Nothing is really final, we can always start over, we can correct our mistakes, we can grow, we can change.

But then there's death, which is forever.

One way to rage against that foreverness is to tell Nomi's story. But the truth is that I cannot tell her story; I can tell only *my* story of her. What I say of her is always true but is never the whole truth. Others saw and knew other truths, a different Nomi. They would (and do) tell different stories. And Nomi is not here to edit any of them or to reconcile the different versions of her life.

Nor, for that matter, is what follows the final truth of my own wrestling with so intimate a death. That wrestling continues; I imagine it will never stop, though its texture changes as the years go by. This is a chronicle of the first five years. The first section, *Real Time,* was written largely as an ongoing diary, as the events it describes unfolded or in their immediate aftermath. Later sections are, for the most part, periodic reflections rather than contemporaneous entries.

Several friends and family members have read this book, in part or in whole, and have offered helpful comments; I am grateful to them all, as also to my editor, Arthur Magida, whose subtle sense of language proved invaluable. I am especially indebted to William Novak, whose tough-minded comments early on helped frame the story I tell, and to Kathleen Peratis: No writer could ask for a more persistent, thoughtful, and generous reader than she, nor for a truer friend.

In the end, as at the beginning, this book is for my granddaughter, Nomi's daughter, Liat.

Preface

SO MUCH OF IT IS A MYSTERY, IS AND WILL EVER SO REMAIN. NOT a puzzle, for a puzzle can finally be solved, even the most brilliantly encrypted code can be deciphered. A mystery.

Why are we here, and for how long, and what is right, and explain, please, love, and art, and is cruelty a mutant gene? These are beyond deciphering, beyond revelation, hidden not at the bottom of the deepest ocean rift, for soon enough our hunt for treasures lost and treasures never known will take us there, nor among the planets or their moons, for soon enough our curiosity and our technology will take us there, but in a fiery chariot that can never be approached or in an ark that is irretrievably lost or in God, unknowable.

We can define infinity, but we cannot comprehend it. Beyond the very largest number there's another, not the last but the next to last. There is no last, not ever, and it is in that next to last, just one beyond our farthest grasp, that the mystery's resolved, clarified.

So we make do with what we have, with what we are given, and yearn.

Yearning has been given to us, a precious gift. We yearn to come closer, and to come deeper, and higher, and to understand, and to accept without needing to understand, and to merge, and to stand alone, and so we plumb the ocean depths and the starry skies, and so we pray, and meditate, and make love, and comfort the wounded.

Oh, the wounded. The legless and the besotted, the widow and the orphan, the burglar and the burgled, all the victims and all the perpetrators, all of us some of the time, some of us all of the time.

We yearn to reenter Eden but with the fruit's acidity intact, not Eden in unselfconscious innocence but Eden hospitable to cleverness and irony and rebellion, to all the forms of our informed disobedience, Eden humanized, God's own Eden II.

But even then and there the mystery remains, for so long as we are human there is death, and so long as there is death there's a boundary, a boundary we cannot cross.

PART I

Real Time:
Life and Death

BOSTON, JANUARY 29, 1996: THE CALL FROM DAVID CAME AT 2:45 that Monday afternoon. Stammering in his panic, he blurted out that Nomi had collapsed, perhaps on account of cardiac arrest, and had been taken to a hospital in Natick, a distant suburb. I called Jessie, youngest at twenty-seven of my three daughters, told her that her sister was in trouble and that I'd pick her up in five minutes—she worked just a few blocks away—then called my friend Sharon with whom I'd been speaking just a minute earlier, told her what had happened, and called the hospital for directions.

Jessie and I stopped for gas before getting on the highway to Natick. I remember thinking as I was pumping the gas that I probably ought to stop after four gallons: If I filled the tank all the way I might be late to the hospital. But the thought was diffuse, reflecting the kind of dark fantasy that parents have and to which I refused to succumb; I filled it all the way. Jessie was trying to calm both of us, thinking out loud that perhaps Nomi had only fainted—she'd done that once or twice before—and we even talked, during the forty-minute trip, about other things. Nomi, after all, had not been sick, not at all; we'd both spoken with her earlier in the day, and there was no premonition of danger. And, improbably, neither of us knew the meaning of cardiac arrest.

We parked in the regular lot rather than the emergency lot and made our way—walking quickly, not running—to the emergency room. I asked after Nomi Fein; the people at the desk asked who I was; I told them I was her father, Jessie her sister, and they took us into a very small room and said the doctor would be with us momentarily. I did not quite "know" yet, although it was plain that something terribly serious was happening; this was not the conventional emergency room response. I asked about Nomi's husband, David—himself a physician—and was told that he, too, would be there very soon. And, in a matter of seconds, before the ominous sense of things had crystallized, David appeared, shuffling, bowed. I looked at him quizzically, and he shook his head in misery. Jessie still didn't fully grasp what had happened, and as she rose from her chair I embraced both her and David and said to her, "She's gone," and the look of stricken terror on her face I shall never forget.

Nomi, dead.

Nomi, alive

When she was six or seven, I began to think her among the most interesting people I'd ever known. "People," not "kids." There was a spiritual depth to her even then, a way she had of dropping back and reflecting that I've never encountered in young children, before or since. "If Jews had nuns," I used to tell my friends, "Nomi would become one."

We don't; she didn't. Instead, she attended the Solomon Schechter Day School, a then-fledgling institution that met in those days in the somewhat ramshackle basement of a synagogue in Newton, a near suburb of Boston. There she flourished, her teachers regularly singing her praises: "Most of us have our 'bad days,'" her fifth-grade teacher wrote, "but it is certainly difficult to think of a day when Nomi has not attended carefully to her academic work, participated sensitively in class discussions, and helped organize her classmates into constructive work and play activities. She has a beautiful spirit that is contagious." This, just a year after her mother and I were divorced.

Academic distinction—a distinction she maintained with very nearly straight A's through college and graduate school—was the lesser part of Nomi's uncommon combination of dazzle and gravity. On April 29, 1978, four months shy of her thirteenth birthday, during the Sabbath service when she became a bat mitzvah, she offered the following commentary on Isaiah 11, the text of the week:

> I feel very lucky to have the *haftorah* portion I have, because within it is one of the most important sentences throughout Jewish history: *V'gar z'ev im keves v'namer im g'di yirbatz, v'egel u'chfir u'mri yachdav v'na'ar katan*

noheg bahm—"and the wolf shall lie down with the lamb, and the leopard shall lie down with the kid, and the calf and the fatling together, and a little child shall lead them."

This passage represents a great hope of the Jewish people from the time we were enslaved in Egypt, continuing through today. Yet as I read this sentence, I cannot help but wonder how the Jews could believe that one day there might be peace when we have seen so much bitterness in our history. Just two weeks ago, many of us watched a recreation of the Holocaust [the 1978 TV miniseries starring Meryl Streep] on television. Watching that, how can we hold on to the hope of peace expressed by Isaiah?

I think that it was important that people watch the show for a second reason also. We have to remember and learn what has happened to us. When one character says to another that the problem of the Jews is that we always remember the past, it is said as an insult. But I think it is a compliment. Yes, the Jews do remember the past. We remember it so that we can be sure never to make the same mistakes twice. But remembering the past is one thing, being enslaved by the past is something else. We remember the past to use it, not to be trapped by it. We cannot be afraid to live fully and happily simply because our past includes so much tragedy. That is how hope can be kept alive alongside of history.

Still, I do not understand the strength of people who know what we know and still can read this sentence from Isaiah and believe in it wholeheartedly. I am not sure that I can read my *haftorah* portion and really believe what I am saying. Perhaps one day I will be able to. Perhaps not only the wolves and the lambs will lie down together, but the hawks and the doves will fly together. Perhaps we will all be able to hope again. Perhaps, even, our hopes for peace will be fulfilled. Perhaps.

We'd watched *Holocaust* together, and talked together about its relationship to her upcoming bat mitzvah and to Isaiah 11. But I wasn't prepared for the impact of these words of a twelve-and-a-half-year-old on a sunny spring day, not for the precocity they indicated nor for the loss of innocence they reflected. (Reading them now, I am struck also by Nomi's easy incorporation of herself into Jewish history: "*We* were enslaved." "*We* have seen." "*We* remember.")

Her bat mitzvah speech speaks to who she was, as years later did her ritual, during her early morning walk to Starbucks with her infant daughter, Liat—in what would turn out to be the last months of Nomi's life—of sitting and chatting for a bit with the homeless schizophrenic man who, most mornings, was parked on a nearby bench.

Back when she was sixteen, and her school gave her a choice of volunteer projects—tutoring new immigrants in English, visiting the elderly, a dozen more—she chose to work at the Ronald McDonald House in Boston, where the parents of kids with cancer stay while their children are being treated at nearby hospitals. The job started out as housekeeping; within a couple of weeks, she was counseling newly arrived parents, was often called to be on hand when they arrived. She didn't talk about it at home; she just did it. And I came to think, and still do, that what seemed at age six or seven to be an unusual spiritual orientation was in fact an uncommon empathic capacity, as if empathy were not merely a trait but a sense, as central as the other five.

So many of the letters of condolence from those who knew her speak to this and related qualities: "There was a special aura about her. Her questions, her sensitive relationship to others. . . ." "I have written hundreds of letters of recommendation for students over the years . . . only a handful were thoughtful enough to respond. I consider myself blessed to have briefly touched her life." "Nomi was not only one of my all-time favorite students and one of the best graduate students I ever had, but she was also one my favorite people. She brought something special to each of us lucky enough to have known her." "She was so interesting and interested." At the end of a handwritten note from Jon-o (long-since become Jon), her close friend in the early years, "I apologize for my spelling but I felt it would be best to be in my natural form without spell check. For many years, Nomi was my spell check. She helped me to cope with my learning disabilities." And so on and so forth, each reminiscence a bittersweet reminder.

It is an easy temptation to embroider the lives of the dead, to portray them as flawless, saintly. I think myself free of that temptation, but even so, I must now and then remind myself that Nomi was, as are we all, imperfect, that she'd take her sister Jessie's clothes without asking and then deny having taken them, that her laugh could be derisive, that she was defensive to a fault. (And yes, it does feel treasonous to write these things now.) Or, less critically, that she also (according to her gym teacher of long ago) "always gave the boys a run for their money. . . . She never let any kind of challenge pass her." But the larger and more glorious truth is that she could feel and write as she did, and elicit from others the reactions she did, that she invested so much in her friendships that there were half a dozen women who thought themselves her best friend, that she could so often (but not always) cause those around her to reach for the better parts of their own nature.

Nomi, dead

The hospital people were most attentive and solicitous. They cleared a somewhat larger room for us, and I called Rachel, eldest of my three daughters. There was no subtle or gradual way to break the awful news, the news that came without any context. She was on another line when I reached her and said she'd call me right back. I told her no, I needed her now, and when she'd dumped the other call I spoke the words: "Rachel, Rachel—Nomi's dead." (Writing now, I want to remember that what I said then was the gentler euphemism, "Nomi's gone." But that would have been pointless, would not have been understood.) And Rachel, of course, broke down immediately, handed the phone to her secretary, who arranged for a car to bring her from downtown Boston, where she works, out to the hospital in Natick, a good twenty miles distant. And then there was Nomi's mother to call, except that she'd lost her husband just a couple of months earlier and we couldn't simply call her. Someone had to go to tell her the news, and none of her close friends was at home, and that left Ruth, my sister-in-law, who is more than adequate for virtually any challenge, even though this one would be especially rough since she and my brother, Rashi, had lost their own thirty-four-year-old daughter, Bena, just the preceding May. And so it was.

The hospital chaplain, in the meanwhile, asked whether we wanted a rabbi, and we did, and water, too, for my throat was so dry I could barely swallow. But no, no tears, not yet, and when Jessie and the nurses and the chaplain and later the rabbi proposed I sit down, meaning that they wanted me to let go, that my apparent stoicism made them nervous, I told them that this—the calls and checking the parking lot for Rachel to arrive and hugging Jessie and the determined not sitting down—was the way I was coping. And the way I wanted to.

Though it had been so sudden, though there had been no warning, no premonition, I felt no shock. Gaping loss, but not shock. Death itself, even untimely death, even the death of a child—these are not, after all, strangers, not to anyone in our century, surely not to a Jew who has internalized the history of his people, who has mourned the distant deaths of children killed by terrorists in Israel, who has, as I did in 1973, stood, crumpled, at Auschwitz. And nothing I had ever learned or believed had led me to believe that I was, that we were, immune. Sure, this is America, my America—I, too young to recall the Great Depression, too young for World War II and Korea, too old for Vietnam—and yes, I'd often thought how charmed we of my family, of this generation, were in specific historical terms, as if we'd slipped into a protected niche where the calamities that have afflicted most generations since the beginning of time, even nature's calamities, happen to others, at a distance. Tornadoes? Trailer parks in Florida and West Virginia. Earthquakes and mudslides? California. Monsoons and tidal waves, plagues and famines, terrorist attacks? All far, very far, away.

Take care to get your kids their shots on schedule, and the boosters; make sure they've had driver ed, that they know about drugs and about drinking and driving; live if you're able where there are no drive-by shootings; and, look around, the odds aren't bad, they're surely in your favor; and yes, here a friend's son is killed by a hit-and-run driver and there someone you know has died in a hotel fire, here a maniac has come after a distant relative with an axe and there a former colleague has died of AIDS; but so far you've been lucky and you're well aware of your good fortune.

Until Bena, last May, my niece who died of an ailment called myelofibrosis, more proximately of a bone marrow transplant that should have worked but didn't, and I said to my kids that's the end of the myth of our family's protected niche, of our insulation from disaster.

So no shock. And, given the circumstances—out of nowhere, Nomi's heart stopped beating—no one to rail against, nor any wisdom to glean. A death with no social significance, with no meaning. I can't take off after drunken drivers, or sue for malpractice, or curse the crime rate. No one killed her; she died, instead, by fluke. The only consolation, then as now, is that Nomi herself did not, does not know, was spared the terror of imminent death, so quickly did she pass from life to death.

All this still in the hospital, with people gathering—my friend Sharon, who'd left for the hospital the moment I called her and arrived only moments after I did; Mark and Eileen, Nomi and David's close friends; and finally Rachel; and then Zelda, Nomi's mom, with my sister-in-law Ruth, who'd brought Zelda; and others, friends of Nomi and David whom I did not know. And decisions, strange decisions for which nothing you've ever done has prepared you: David's—no postmortem; yes, the organs would be donated; yes, Rabbi Elkin, headmaster at the Schechter school, would be asked to officiate at the funeral. And mine—my first conversation with the funeral home: How's Wednesday at one?; yes, a notice in the *Globe*; yes, in keeping with the tradition, a *shomer,* someone to sit with Nomi, reciting psalms, until the funeral. And all the while, the hospital staff hovering. And Jessie trembling, trembling.

Life without Nomi?

Nomi, alive

Alongside Nomi's empathy, a sometimes frighteningly deli-
cate sensitivity: A mere hint of criticism from me was enough
to provoke tears, criticism from others enough to provoke an
unseemly defensiveness. Families stumble into myths, and
the myths provide guidelines, and living according to their
guidelines solidifies the myths. Nomi, our myth went, was my
favorite, my soulmate. The myth conveniently overlooked
how bound up I was with Rachel, our firstborn, how much I
felt indebted to her for having taught me by her sheer presence in my life so much about my gentler side, how much I
respected her for toughing it out in the aftermath of her parents' divorce, how much I admired her work ethic. And later,
much later, as Jessie and I became partners in various projects
and as I came to appreciate her wit and her wisdom—the
Nomi-as-favorite myth ran out of supporting energy.

Still, there was a time, a decade or more, when the myth
shaped and then roughly fit the facts. Parents have different
expectations of their children, and as I now reflect on these
matters, it seems to me that my expectation was that Nomi,
more than the other two, would understand me—understand
(perhaps also share?) my convictions, understand also my
confusions. And she was the most overtly intellectual of the
three, the one with the voracious intellectual appetite: At my
own alma mater, the University of Chicago, a few months into
her freshman year, she announced that she wanted to do a
triple major—anthropology, music, and religion—so that she
could work on the origins of sacred music. (The combined
interest didn't last, but she did end up majoring in anthropology, then went on to Northwestern with a handsome graduate

fellowship from the National Institute of Mental Health.) But it wasn't—I don't think—that I saw myself in her more than in the others, or that—as the others sometimes suggested (and even now propose)—she was "most like me."

Reading through the reminiscences and the tributes that arrived in the weeks after her death, I have come to understand that I was simply her fan, perhaps her most enthusiastic fan, responding to the same qualities that so many others discerned and described.

Her obstetrician, for example, in a letter to Liat after Nomi died:

> I saw your mother in my office very frequently. Many days I would be running late and the patients had to wait. Some of the women would get mad at me, but not your mom. I would come into the room to see her, and rather than tell me about her aches and pains, she would ask me how I was doing. I would instantly feel more calm. . . . When I arrived at my office the day after you were born, there were flowers on my desk. Your parents had sent them to celebrate your birth.

"When a child dies," I started to write here, and then realized that this is not about an abstract child, it is about this child, about Nomi. So: When Nomi died, I searched through the "kids" directory in my computer and found there letters I'd written to her over the years. (They're addressed to "Skeeps," my name for her, derived from the days when I bounced her on my knee while chanting, "Nomsky Pomsky Jeepers Skeepers.") Here is one example of what it meant to be her fan, written on the occasion of her nineteenth birthday:

August 22, 1984

Skeeps:

I thought about dazzling you with a rented plane pulling a "Happy Birthday, Nomi" banner, and I probably could have arranged it, and it would have been fun, but, apart from the expense, which would have been considerable, there's also the simple fact that that wouldn't have begun to express my good wishes for you as you turn nineteen. (Nineteen! Wow!)

'Cause what I really want to say by way of happy birthday wishes is about other stuff, the mushy stuff that's best said in letters because in person it gets a bit sticky.

So, some mushy stuff: Kids don't exist to make their parents proud. I have to remind myself that that's not your job in life; it is an incidental by-product. But my, what a by-product! Your combination of talent and sensitivity and energy and intellect is a constant delight to me, and I thank you for such delights, really thank you.

You've grown, too fast, into a young womanhood that gives every sign of being what I suspected it would be back when you were six or seven and I said to myself, "This little person Nomi is one of the most interesting people I've ever known." And now, with a record of success behind you, and a world wide open in front of you, my birthday wish for you is that you go from strength to strength, from success to success, that these next few years be marked by your continuing self-discovery and your increasingly coherent use of your vast abilities. Skeeps, you've got it all; all the parts are there. The next chapter will be about fitting those parts together into an adult life, and making some of the hard choices all of us have to make about the directions of that life. But you are a person who can, and, I have no doubt, will make the life you choose; life will not 'happen' to you, you will not be its passive receptacle. It's going to be fun to watch, and to be a minor participant in, the unfolding, given the splendid beginning.

So, finally, on this, your nineteenth birthday, what I really want to say is thank you—for all these good years, truly good years, past. May every step of your way be marked with meaning and with delight; may the pain that is part of life be eased by the pride you feel in your accomplishments, and in what you mean to those who love you; may your choices be wise and productive, and may your mistakes be rare and reversible; may the light and the warmth and the sheer pleasure you have brought to me be your own companions all the days of your life. And may God continue to bless you and to keep you, to make His countenance shine upon you, and grant you peace.

Written, and sent, with all my love.

I cite that letter here for a double purpose: First, to indicate the texture of my feelings towards this child, and, second, because it has become exceedingly important to me to know that my expression of love is not a postmortem inflation, but was fully shared when it mattered, that I said it in time. And more than once. Among my dark, my brooding imaginings: We fought, and she died before we repaired the breach. But there was no such fight, not then, not, as nearly as I can recall, ever.

That sounds preposterous, I know. Perhaps it is a trick of memory, her death a filter that does not let the bad stuff in. I do not think so—but with whom shall I now check my sense of how it was between us? So why doubt my memory? It is enough that it consoles, and I will clasp it to me as I will and do any and all consolation. That, I suppose, is why my old letters have become so important to me.

I cannot, based on this tragic experience, advise my friends who are parents that they take care of their children; Nomi was cared for, and that wasn't enough. The one piece of advice I've felt qualified to pass on to other parents these past weeks is precisely: Make sure you let your kids know, each day, how much you care for them, love them. I've said that to friends and to strangers, to cabdrivers and salespeople and seatmates on airplanes, said it to them with a sense of urgency: Now, do it now, before—may God forbid—it is too late.

Perhaps that's too somber. Under the circumstances, what people will understand is that I am calling attention to the fact that we can never know what day will be ours or our children's last. But it is not so ominous an ongoing awareness I mean to propose, let alone impose. What I really mean to say is that in all our important relationships, we should try as best we can to keep up-to-date, to leave no (or very few) ends dangling, and with our children, our most important relationship, all the more so. And the reason is not—or not only—that our children may die before nightfall (even though it is obviously that experience that has prompted this caution) or that we ourselves may, but that some other frightful circumstance may make it impossible for us to say to them the things we feel most keenly, things that left unsaid, or unheard, may occur to us to say only too late. Too late.

"This child," I wrote above. The growth from little-girlhood into womanhood—I would not call it a blossoming, because the four- and five-year-old is already a blossoming flower—is a piece of magic. It takes place before our eyes, and yet we cannot see it while it is happening. Perhaps a mother is more attuned to the stages, to the marks along the way. In any case, I rather suspect that every father, at least in societies such as ours where marriage typically happens sometime after adolescence, wonders on the day of her marriage what happened, and when, to the little girl he once carried piggyback. Turn around, she's a woman; turn around once more, she's a mother.

When David ushered us into the delivery room to meet our granddaughter, it was not Liat Gabrielle I noticed, it was Nomi. ("Liat" is a Hebrew name—pronounced "lee-aht"—which means "you're mine.") "Noticed" may be the wrong word: Of course I saw the newborn, but it was the larger context that thrilled me, the sight of Liat nestled in the crook of Nomi's arm: my child become a mother, instantly a generation older. (As had I, by extension.) It was that consciousness that stayed with me for all the months to come, the months that were left. I never felt what grandfathers are "supposed" to feel. Liat was (and is), of course, beautiful beyond belief, and bright, and all the rest, but it wasn't she who was the center of my attention. When Nomi and Liat came to visit me, or I them, it was Nomi-as-mommy who fascinated me. (Even when, as was the case especially in the early months, I'd bite my tongue a dozen times a visit. Given all that she'd read about infants, given, I also imagine, the fact that David's a doctor specializing in family medicine, Nomi wasn't exactly eager to hear my advice on whether Liat was dressed too warm, too cold, whatever.)

Oh, how she loved the baby, the effort she put into planning each day (the morning stroll to Starbucks, and then off to a play area somewhere, and, in the afternoon, a visit to the Children's Museum or to the home of a friend with an infant child), the enthusiasm with which she reported on Liat's development and the glee with which she described her own feelings of love and attachment. One day, just weeks before her death, we spoke by phone. Perhaps she heard an edge in my voice—I was beginning to wonder when, even whether, she'd start looking for work—as I asked, "What did you do today?" Her answer, immediate: "I helped Liat get a day older."

Nomi, dead

Away from the hospital, finally. Gathering, our numbers expanding, at the house, at Nomi and David's house. Trying again and again to reach David's parents, who live in London, Ontario. Other calls, to the close friends and family members. Zoe, Nomi's good friend, nine full months pregnant, due that very day, who had been with her own child and with Nomi and Liat when Nomi collapsed, who had taken Liat home with her when Nomi was taken to the hospital, Zoe bringing sixteen-month old Liat home, and everyone in the by-then crowded house tightening up at the sight of this suddenly motherless child. David plainly in shock, virtually catatonic. Waiting for Rabbi Elkin, who will come after the Schechter School board meeting, a meeting that Nomi, a member of the board, had been scheduled to attend.

Earlier that day, I'd been listening to some CDs that I'd bought in Israel the week before, recordings of Israeli and Jewish music I'd intended to distribute to my children. The listening was meant to enable me to decide which CD should go to whom. I'd started with a recording of Hassidic music, and when I heard on it a rendition of the Rabbi Nachman of Bratslav song, I knew that record would be for Nomi and David. The song: "The whole world is a very narrow bridge, and the main thing is not to be at all afraid."

Later I would learn that when Josh Elkin opened the Schechter board meeting, he told the people there that he had some hard news to share with them. Before telling them of Nomi's death—knowing nothing of my CD—he said, "Let me start by quoting the words of a song by Nachman of Bratslav: 'The whole world is a very narrow bridge, and the main thing is not to be at all afraid.'" (From coincidence to intention: And that is why the funeral service would begin with the singing of that song.)

And the house, of course, filled with Nomi. The couch on which she spent so much of her pregnancy during the months when bed rest was prescribed for her. The mementos of Nepal and the other places she and David visited during their six-month trek around the world, the trip they'd planned to take even before they were married but that was postponed once the problem with Nomi's heart was discovered, the problem that would eventually lead to the insertion of a pacemaker, a pacemaker that was supposed to take care of the problem. "An unusual problem in a person so young," we'd been told, "but not to worry: The pacemaker will take care of it." And it did. The pacemaker functioned perfectly right through the end. It's just that somewhere behind the problem the pacemaker solved there was evidently another, darker problem, one that was never discerned, a pathology that would cause her heart to stop on a Monday afternoon in January while she was playing with her baby.

There's a clinical name for the cause of Nomi's death. I have heard it more than once, but I do not know it. It adds nothing, changes nothing. I have inquired to determine whether Rachel or Jessica, Nomi's sisters, or Liat, her daughter, are in any related way at risk, and the doctors assure me they are not. That is all the clinical information that matters.

Rashi and Ruth, my brother and sister-in-law, had called some of the out-of-towners, and each call elicited the same stunned response: "Nomi? What Nomi? What are you saying?" For there was simply no context, even for those who knew of the pacemaker. It had been different with Bena: She'd been sick, life-threateningly sick, and there'd been time to adjust to the gravity of her condition. But at no point had anyone viewed Nomi as in any way incapacitated. She'd come into a room loaded with bundles, and no one would rush to relieve her of her burden. Not one of the physicians who'd treated her had advised caution; on the contrary, they'd promised total normalcy. (The bed rest during her pregnancy was for other and unrelated reasons.)

And finally, dispersal to our several homes, leaving David and Liat with their friends Mark and Eileen, who would spend the night in what was still and would remain for many weeks Nomi and David's house. And I, not yet ready—afraid—to return to my home, where I live alone, off to Rashi and Ruth's, to whom I was now and forever connected in this new and utterly absurd way. We were joined there by their son, Alan, who years earlier had lost his fiancée to cervical cancer. I do not know how long we sat, nor have I even a hazy recollection of what we spoke about. I remember only that while sitting there, two friends from California, searching for me, called. The news had already crossed the continent.

About midnight, I went home. Rashi and Ruth had asked whether I wanted to stay in their guest room, others volunteered to spend the night with me at my place. But I am used to being alone, was ready now to be alone, was numb. The shock had settled in.

Nomi, alive

Every person's biography begins before he or she is born. A family tree is not merely a chart, it is a prelude, and if we take the trouble to do more than simply list the names along the way, if we find out what we can about our progenitors, then we know something of who we were before we took on a physical presence, before we took on the specific shape that we recognize in the mirror, before we came to the consciousness we define as life. And why limit our inquiry, our origins, to our genetic predecessors? What of their neighbors, what of the land, the air, the folk?

I had lunch yesterday with Arnie, whose father was wounded while fighting with the Lincoln Brigade during the Spanish Civil War. The offending bullet missed being fatal by some three inches. Bad aim, or a speck of dust in the sniper's eye at the critical moment, and because of a speck of dust, there came eventually to be an Arnie for me to have lunch with yesterday. What is it the theory of chaos teaches us? When a butterfly moves its wings somewhere in China, the chain of consequences reaches to our own doorstep. Begin that way and all explanation is rendered impossible, so dense is the causal nexus. But know nonetheless that what Arnie's grandfather read, and the stories Arnie's father's colleagues told when the battle calmed (which means among other things what their grandfathers read, which means in turn what others, some in far distant times and places, wrote) are part of who Arnie is.

Nomi was a descendent of a man known as the Ba'al Shem Tov, Master of the Good Name, who in the first part of the eighteenth century founded a Jewish religious movement called Hasidism. In our family, we learned that the Ba'al Shem Tov had promised to be present at the weddings of his descendants until the tenth generation—and Nomi was, as Rachel and Jessie are, that tenth generation. I'd told the story to Nomi, and she had told it to her friend, Mychal, who co-officiated at Nomi and David's wedding—and would so few years later eulogize Nomi at her funeral.

When Mychal charged the newlyweds, this (in part) is what she said:

> You know, of course, that the Ba'al Shem Tov promised to be here today, and I think all of us can feel his presence in the warmth and the love that is so much a part of this day. But plainly, the promise begets a question: What happens in the eleventh generation? And what I want to say is that while what the Ba'al Shem Tov promised was that he would be present through the tenth generation, he did not mean to say that he would not be present after that. He only implied that he wasn't going to commit in advance for the generations beyond the tenth. Which means that in the eleventh generation, in the generation of your children, Nomi and David, his presence depends on the kind of home you build together.

If your biography begins before you're born, then it includes the dreams of those who came before. And if it includes those dreams, and if those dreams become part of who you are and are therefore passed along to those whose lives yours touches, then your biography goes on after you return to the dust. Life, as we understand it, is about consciousness; that's how we come by the idea of "brain dead." But consciousness is not a "thing," something you have or don't have; it is an unfolding and ever-changing process. And though my consciousness will one day come to an end, its consequences continue. Indeed, the very term "my consciousness" is somewhat misleading, since so much of who I am began before and outside me, just as who I have managed to become will enter and affect the lives of others.

Perhaps this is easier to grasp if we drop the word "consciousness" and substitute for it the word "story." A person's story begins before the person's born; if the story is richly lived, it infects a hundred other people's stories, and theirs a thousand more.

In Nomi's case, the most obvious consequence of Nomi's consciousness, the most obvious sequel to Nomi's story—but hardly the only one—is Liat, her daughter.

We worry now about Liat. Not about her welfare or her prospects of growing up lively, alert, delightful. No, our worry is more specific, more selfish: Will Liat, only sixteen months old when her mother died, be Nomi's daughter always? The worry is very nearly instinctive, and is a way of expressing our need for Nomi to live, somehow. (But it is not wholly selfish; it is also a recognition of Nomi's special qualities, of our hope that these have been passed on to Liat—and our fear that nature without nurture will prove inadequate for their transmission.)

Two weeks after the death, David and I took Liat to the Children's Museum, and she crawled happily about. She came to a giant photograph of a family—a mother, a father, several children—and turned to us: "Mommy?"

Odds are that some day, Liat will call someone else "mommy." We have to hope for that, and do. But we want, very much, that she will know and honor the woman who gave her birth and loved her so. At Nomi's funeral, we asked the rabbi to speak these words:

> One day we will need—and want—to tell Liat about her mom. It would mean a great deal to all of us, and most of all to Liat, if those of you who knew Nomi would write down some of your own memories of her, of the times you spent together, of the ways she touched your life, of the joys and the sadnesses and all that made her so very, very special, and send them along to Liat's grandparents or her sisters or her dad.

And the children's psychiatrist whom David consulted not long after Nomi died said yes, by all means, show Nomi's picture to Liat, and show the videos, tell her Nomi stories so that Nomi becomes part of her consciousness. Weeks later, we know he is right: Now and then Liat will suddenly frown, put her hands in front of her, palms up, and say, "Mommy . . . gone." And on the floor in a corner of her room, with David's help, she has made a space for framed photographs of her mother, and sometimes plays there, quietly.

There was a moment, in the hospital, as I watched David sobbing, that I wished there'd been no issue from the marriage. (Interesting, I think, the euphemisms with which we distance the unthinkable: Suddenly, Liat is "issue.") How much simpler David's life would now be. But the moment passed quickly, displaced by the knowledge of how much joy Nomi experienced with and through Liat in what would prove to be the last sixteen months of her life. And now, weeks later, knowing also that Liat is David's anchor, knowing so much better—for in our hovering, we've all spent more time with Liat than before—the laughter and the pride and the simple pleasure Liat evokes, no shadow of doubt that she's a blessing.

Still, a blessing that is joined to a burden.

And because David is not who David was before Nomi entered his life, and because I am not who I was, because all of us are who we are in smaller or in larger part in consequence of Nomi's thirty years, Liat's story will necessarily be shaped by Nomi's.

Too simple, that. It is not Nomi's voice that will sing Liat to sleep or read her bedtime tales; it is not Nomi who will teach her courtesy and kindness. She will learn these things, but she will not be quite (or even nearly?) who she would have been, even if she is, as we hope and mean to encourage, quite wonderful.

So yes, there are stories that extend beyond the grave, and those stories include not only Liat; they reach to a remarkably large number of people who knew and were affected by Nomi. My friend and former student, Steve, tells me that on the streets of Jerusalem the day after Nomi died, people who knew he was my friend came up to him to talk about Nomi, to tell him of her impact on their lives. He wishes, he now says, he'd listened better to the Nomi stories I'd told him over the years, wishes he'd known Nomi. (Steve learned of what had happened from a mutual friend. She'd called, he tells me, asking whether he'd heard about me. From her voice, Steve understood that something was wrong, and he thought, fearing the worst, that something awful had happened to me. He sat down, and then she told him about Nomi, and he realized that there is worse than the worst.) In California, where Nomi went to summer camp and later worked as a camp counselor, and in Jerusalem, where she worked for two years as a volunteer (and where she met David), and here in Boston, too, at the Schechter school she attended, there's talk of setting up funds in her memory. Consequences, and they come as a comfort, they enable me to place these ruminations under the heading, "Nomi, alive."

But it is a comfort encased in ice.

Nomi, dead

Wednesday, the day of the funeral. It is snowing.

Sharon comes to be with me. Years ago, we were ever so briefly married. Since then, we have been sometime-partners and always-friends. This week, she is my rock. Other friends, from New York and from Los Angeles, will arrive over the course of the morning, weather permitting. I call Rachel, then Jessie; Jessie says, simply: "How are we going to do this?" Save to tell her that somehow we will, that we have no choice, I have no answer.

Nomi will be buried next to her cousin, Bena, in a plot that was to have been mine. Next to them, my parents, confused beyond belief, I imagine, by the out-of-sequence arrival of their progeny. At the funeral home, yesterday, I made the necessary arrangements—the number of limousines (three), the number of police escorts (four), the nature of the casket (in keeping with the tradition, a plain pine box); Sharon took notes. Sharon also answered for me when I was asked the one question I could not bring myself to answer on Nomi's behalf, on behalf of this person with whom I'd gone shopping for clothing countless times, with whom I'd haunted The Gap and Saks Fifth Avenue, with whom on a visit to the Polo outlet store in Zurich I'd splurged quite recklessly on her stateside wardrobe: Shall her shroud be of linen or of muslin?

Now Sharon reminds me that the check for the cemetery is due today. But I prepare my checks on the computer, and the computer program requires that each check be assigned to a category. To what category can I assign this check? It does not belong with "miscellaneous," and I cannot put it with "kids," there where I have ten years and more of my letters to my children. A new category? I cannot write the words: Funeral? Burial? Until now I have been adequately responsive, but to write such words is to confirm what has happened, and I cannot.

I call my brother, who uses the same check-writing program, my brother who buried his daughter nine months ago. He tells me, matter-of-factly, that the costs will continue for a while, and that I'd best make a category. His category, in his typically straightforward way, is "funeral." Again, I am responsive. And so "funeral" now happens in my Quicken directory between "entertainment" and "gifts."

My friends—Rachel, Pam, Irv and Susan, Lucie—arrive, Pam with an assortment of comfort food from Zabar's in New York. Earlier, I've said to Sharon that one of the burdens of this day will be all the hugging. I am not from the California-style huggers; I prefer selective hugging. But these are my friends, and their hugs are welcome.

I pick a suit to wear. It is a new suit, just back from the tailor. And a tie. Tradition has it that the mourners wear a black ribbon, pinned on their clothing just before the funeral and cut with a razor blade, the contemporary evocation of the ancient rending of one's clothing. Josh Elkin, who will officiate, has told us that he finds the ribbon-cutting too removed, that he prefers an actual garment, an actual rending. The women—Rachel and Jessie, and Zelda, Nomi's mother—opt for the ribbon. David and I accept Josh's advice, and I pick a tie that will in just an hour's time be ripped, destroyed.

Until this morning, I thought to eulogize my daughter. Who else can be depended on to frame her life, to specify our loss? And I have, over the years, acquired the necessary experience as a eulogist, most recently of Bena. Rashi and Ruth have urged me not to speak today; it will be too hard, they say, and it is not fair to those assembled, who will be wondering whether I will be able to do it, worrying that I will break down during the doing of it. Later, I will understand that they were right. But this morning it is something else that leads me to choose silence.

I am a public person. I am used to audiences, comfortable with them. And though my speeches and my lectures are hardly theatrical, there is inherently an element of performance about them. I cannot trust myself to ad lib a eulogy; if I am to speak for Nomi, I will have to write out what I want to say, and I will, because that is how I do such things, hunt for just the right word, the fitting turn of phrase. But this morning, I am in touch with myself in a way I have been only once before, on the day twenty-three years ago when I visited Auschwitz. There, too, I was silent; without the mask of words, authentic. I feel that unstudied authenticity this morning, and welcome it. There will come time for words, and need. (Are these not those words?) But this day is not that time, not for my own sake, not for Nomi's. Let others, if they are so disposed, seek to decorate her death, to mediate it. I must be free to feel, to weep.

Also, I am exhausted.

It is time to go.

Nomi, alive

We went to Israel together once, the girls and I. It was the best of times. I'd promised them a genuine tourists' trip, no meetings or conferences, and so (with just one or two exceptions) it was. We went to Yad VaShem, Israel's principal memorial to the Holocaust, and one moonlit night, we climbed historic Masada, just the four of us (thirty-seven minutes from bottom to top, absurdly less challenging than we'd been cautioned it would be), and promptly fell asleep atop the desert mesa, sleeping right through the fabled sunrise. We traveled to kibbutzim in the north and to development towns in the south. And in Jerusalem, we visited Miriam Mendelow at her Lifeline for the Elderly, a place where the elderly work at diverse crafts in order to maintain their independence. Miriam, who died a few years later, was one of those storied people of near-obsessive passion who had created something out of nothing. She believed, simply, that old people shouldn't be discarded. So she fashioned an alternative, a series of workshops where the elderly disabled could work, where Arabs and Jews could share a workbench, where ancient crafts could be preserved, where dignity could be protected and defended.

On our last night in the country, a cousin asked what, of all the things they'd seen, had impressed my daughters most. I expected them to say Yad VaShem; there, I'd tried, protectively, to move them along, but they insisted on a slower pace, wanted to read the legend under each of the photographs that chronicle our people's calamity. It is hard to imagine a place more disturbingly evocative than Yad VaShem. Or, perhaps, I thought, they'll pick Masada, our good-humored anticlimax overshadowed by this desert hilltop where Herod had his winter palace and where, more memorably, Eliezer ben Ya'ir 2000 years ago urged his people to end their lives rather than surrender to the Romans who besieged them.

But no, it was Lifeline for the Elderly they chose, all three of them. And it was Nomi who explained: Yes, Yad VaShem is terribly moving, but in this generation, in our generation, the forces of evil have been muffled, and we are not invited to martyrdom. And yes, Masada is a chunk of history, but we are not today besieged. Lifeline, on the other hand, is an invitation: In this generation, what we are asked to do is to spend a week, or a summer, or whatever, as volunteers in a place that makes life a bit easier for people.

Three years later, Nomi was off to Israel on her own, at last a break from four years of Dean's List work at the University of Chicago and a year earning her Master's at Northwestern. A year to volunteer, to make life a bit easier, and richer, for people. On the eve of her departure, I wrote to her:

July 12, 1988

Skeeps:
The mushy stuff you already know—how much I love you, how much I believe in you, how high are my hopes for you, how much joy and pride you have given me. If you are only half as pleased with yourself as I am pleased with you, you're in danger of being intolerably smug and conceited. (But among the things I notice about you, with delight, is your apparent utter lack of conceit.)

I was younger than you when I first spent a year in Israel. It was 1953, and I had just turned nineteen.

And I was (as I now remember it) so interested in impressing people that I never asked any questions about anything. (That way, people would think I already knew everything. I didn't.) So: Ask questions. Find out how much bread costs. Find out what goes on in an Israeli classroom. Try to understand people from the inside out. Think big cultural and semiotic thoughts, and also tiny thoughts. Enter everything with a combination of your usual verve and enthusiasm, but also with your anthropological skills and perspectives. Make peace in the Middle East, or, at least, in your neighborhood.

Do this, do that, do everything. Be careful. Be smart. (I don't have to take time to tell you to be good; that you will be because you cannot help it. The other stuff—careful and smart—may take remembering.)

Keep your journal. Write it for yourself, but make it good enough so Pam can sell it and you can make a million dollars and support me in the style to which I would like to become accustomed.

Be careful.

Write to me. Often, but not more than daily. Do not call collect; it is wildly more expensive, I think (but maybe you should check on that.) Have fun. Remember that Israeli women your age (as also men) have been in the army. Spend time with your cousin Segal; you can learn from her. You can learn from everyone. (But do not spend time with everyone. There's not enough time.) Learn Arabic. Learn Hebrew. Learn Israel. Learn life. Be careful.

My friends—Uzi and Haim in particular, but Matt and Yossi and the others—will always be available if you need them. That's what friends are for.

Come home.

As I stood at the dock (I went by boat) in 1953—my god, thirty-five years ago!—my father took me aside and gave me a rare hug, blurting out "Hitch your wagon to a star," or some such. Your wagon's already hitched; keep the connections tight. I know that you've got a good grasp on goodness. How much else—stardom not only as a mentsh, which is the most important, but also in your work—you can bring off, I don't know. But I wouldn't discount the possibility that you have major contributions to make in your work. Still, and always, the Nobel Prize itself pales in comparison to the importance of *mentshlichkeit* [being a mentsh; humaneness]. That remains both your legacy and your distinctive skill.

In Israel, Nomi volunteered here and worked part-time there and found and attached herself to a group of professors at the Hebrew University who were working in a new field called "media education." In Israel she met David, who'd come there from Canada thinking to stay. But they fell in love, and Nomi stayed on for a second year, and then they came back, first for a year to Toronto, and then here, to Boston.

As I write these words, the radio brings news that two terrorist bombs have exploded in Israel, killing twenty-seven people, twenty-five of them on a bus in Jerusalem. These are the first such attacks in some months, and they remind us that a peace process is not yet peace. They remind me not to be lulled into a false sense of safety, that when I turn on the radio in the morning, I must still hold my breath as the first headlines are announced: Have we made it through the night in safety?

Too often, far too often, we have not. Israel—its travails and its heady accomplishments—have been part of my life since I was a youngster. I do not, never have, filed what happens there under "foreign affairs." Israel, in short, is not an abstraction for me, nor has it been for my children. Nomi might have been on that bus. Other people were, other people's children were.

Indeed, the phone rings within the hour with the news that among this morning's dead is Yoni Barnea, the son of my friends Nahum and Tammy, with whom I spent my last evening in Israel just a month ago, from whom I received a condolence letter just days after Nomi died. And now I shall have to write to them, and to the Eisenfelds and Dukers, too, parents of the two young Americans among the twenty-seven dead. Suddenly, we are all part of the same grim fraternity, the fraternity our tradition calls "the rest of the mourners of Zion and Jerusalem," among whom we are "to be comforted."

And yet: Is it envy I now feel, envy for Nahum and Tammy, whose son has been martyred, whose death unlike Nomi's has both cause and context, is part of a larger story rather than merely evidence of the random, the absurd?

Nomi, dead

I arrive at the funeral home. Sharon is with me; my other visitors are coming in Irv's rented car. The manager of the home greets us; we are the first to arrive. He takes my coat and leads me to the chapel. There is the casket. The *shomer,* reciter of psalms, withdraws discretely, and I am alone. Alone with the box, before which I kneel, on which I place my head, and I stroke the box. If I do not leave it, leave her, time will stop. There will be no funeral, no burial. If there is no burial, she is not dead.

But the box I am stroking is made of wood.

I leave, return to the family room. Others in the family begin to arrive, and soon thereafter, friends. And here is cousin Saul, who has flown up from Florida; and Andrea, stepsister to my daughters, who has come from Israel; and Natalie and Aaron, Nomi's friends, who have flown in from Los Angeles and will return home immediately after the burial; their new baby is just eighteen days old. Word of the tragedy traveled very fast, carried as if by jungle drums to distant places, close friends. Now, many of them are here. Some stop in the family room to pay their respects. Most go directly to the chapel, and I will not learn until after they have left that they were here.

It is time for the *kriyah,* the rending of the garment—or the ribbon. Zelda and Rachel and Jessie and Andrea receive their ribbons, and the ribbons are cut. The funeral director approaches David, takes hold of the lapel of his suit—it is his wedding suit—and makes the cut, then tells him to take both hands and rip. David does. Then he comes to me, and I cannot bring myself to say, "No, just the tie, please." He cuts, I rip, and the ripping of the suit feels right. It is not a ripping but a rending. This is my garment, now ruined. It matches what has happened inside me.

And now we must enter the chapel, sit in its front row, a few feet from the casket. I see, as we enter, that all the seats are filled, that people are standing against the walls. Only later will I learn that the overflow room is also filled, that some 500 people have come to mourn the passing of the young woman who is/was my daughter, some because they knew and loved her, others because they know and love one or another of us, the bereaved. This pleases me, not only on account of personal vanity (yes, even now there is that) but because it confirms that something important has happened, something that has shaken a whole community and not just a diminished family.

The service begins. Psalms are read, and then our friend Moshe Waldoks sings the Nachman of Bratslav song with its challenging words: "The whole world is a very narrow bridge, and the main thing is not to be afraid at all." I am glad the congregation that has here assembled includes enough people who know the song—it is not all that widely known—so that his is not a solo performance. Eileen, Nomi's dear friend, who will later take an extended leave of absence from her job so she can help with Liat, rises to eulogize her friend; her husband, Mark, is at her side to help her make it through her tearful presentation.

And then Mychal, Nomi's best friend through childhood, Mychal whom I have known and loved since she was six or seven and both our neighbor and Nomi's classmate at Schechter. Mychal now grown up, now a rabbi, the very rabbi who officiated at Nomi and David's wedding, Mychal who remembers their years together and speaks at length of Nomi's magic. No one stands next to her, although she is a tiny slip of a woman and her eyes are brimming. But her voice does not waver and she captures Nomi. She describes how people were drawn to her, wanting to experience her magic, how after school she and Nomi would walk the streets of Brookline singing Hebrew songs, singing each a dozen times before they'd move on to the next, how towards supper time one would walk the other home, and then the other would walk the first one home, and then again, until they'd run out of daylight. She described Nomi's "rare talent" of being simultaneously "a kids' kid and an adults' kid," the teachers loving her for her creativity and inspiring intelligence, the kids for her natural leadership and her magic. She knew, Mychal says, how to get along with everyone. (A middle child's special gift?) And she reminisced: the time around the dinner table when Nomi's grandmother, Zelda's mother, talked about sex with her husband, shocking Zelda and the two girls alike; the time the two of them came to my house to help prepare the gefilte fish for Passover; the years they drifted apart and their coming back during the year both were in Israel; their conversation on what would be Nomi's last birthday, talking about the "incredible blessings" in Nomi's life, of David and Liat, about how much richer and fuller their lives were than they'd ever guessed they would be, about how close they felt to each other and how much they looked forward to the many years of friendship that lay ahead.

And then Josh Elkin, who says what so obviously wants saying, that this Nomi was the ideal graduate of an American Jewish day school, involved in her own community, concerned and involved with the larger world, and that we are all diminished by her death.

And the time I have been apprehensively awaiting draws near: The centerpiece of a Jewish funeral is the mournful chanting of the *El Molei Rachamim* ["God Full of Compassion"], and the ancient prayer is always personalized to include the name(s) of the deceased, so-and-so the son/daughter of [father's given name] and [mother's given name], the names, as the prayer itself, in Hebrew, and I am about to hear my daughter's name, and mine, so chanted.

My mother died when she was seventy-eight, my father when he was eighty-nine, both in the fullness of time. My mother, Chaya the daughter of Shlomo and Rivka, was born to parents I never knew, parents who died in the Old Country. When the names of her parents were chanted at her funeral, they were already, as is proper, long gone. So, too, my father's parents, Matya and Meir, who made it to America but who, long before my father died, had been gathered to their ancestors. But I am Nomi's ancestor, and I am standing here, and as Moshe Waldoks nears the terrible line that makes this a prayer for Nomi, daughter of Leibel and Zelda, I hold tight to the people on either side of me, bring their hands to my chest.

Nomi, dead

I am so glad I cannot see the end of the cars in the cortege as we head to the cemetery. I have been on this route before; it seems much, much longer now. I watch the police escort with fascination, as on motorcycles they lap each other to block off every upcoming intersection. It has stopped snowing. There are folding chairs for the bereaved. It is very cold, and I have left my coat in the car. The casket rests on straps over the emptiness below. Bena's grave is rudely covered by the earth that will fill Nomi's. The casket is lowered; I whisper, "Gently, gently." Josh Elkin nods to me and to David; we rise, approach the grave, he at one end and I at the other, take hold of the shovels, and begin. In our tradition, this work is for us and our friends to do, not for strangers. I try, vainly, to let the earth slide off the shovel softly, even tenderly. But the grave is deep, and the sound of the earth hitting the casket is a bitter punctuation mark: Now begins the ending, the real ending.

My child is being buried.

We return the shovels to the mound; others approach, retrieve them, continue to fill the grave. (The tradition instructs: Do not hand the shovel to the next person; return it to the earth, lest you seem in too great a hurry to complete the work.) It is bitter cold; there is snow in the air. Sharon stands behind me, slips my coat, which she has retrieved from the car, over my shoulders. I watch as Rachel and Jessie spill earth into their sister's grave, onto their sister's casket. I can see that they, too, are stunned by the heaviness of the earth's fall.

Slowly, the grave is filled, and slowly, Bena's grave comes into view. And then once again the *El Molei Rachamim,* and once again the mourner's kaddish, the solemn prayer of the bereaved that we will now recite with Nomi in mind for the rest of our lives. Josh reads psalms, something to do with God as the True Judge, and I shake my head, no, these words are preposterous: They lie. It is time to leave. For a moment, Rashi and I stand together, alone, at our daughters' graves. We do not speak. What is there to say?

The congregation forms two lines through which we pass. Zelda, from whom I was divorced in 1974, walks to one side of David, I to the other, an inescapable reminder of the aisle we walked just yesterday when Nomi and David were married. In the Jewish tradition, if a funeral cortege and a wedding parade bump into each other along the way, it is the funeral cortege that must stand aside.

Nomi, dead

There is no wedding parade today. There are only the limousines, now liberated from their funereal pace, bringing us back to Nomi and David's where others will have seen to the food. Along the way, I indulge myself: Maybe there is an afterlife?

This is the first magical thinking I have engaged in; it will not be the last. The whole thing's a hoax: Nomi is hiding somewhere. It was our divorce that damaged her heart, and that is why this happened. It was something else, a sin committed long ago, long ago forgotten. At the end of days, we shall have a reunion. She is looking down on us from above.

Somewhere, somehow, there must be a logic to all this; it must fit. One late evening, weeks later, the phone rings. I pick it up, and though the line is open, no one responds to my repeated "hello." I hang up the phone—and begin to tremble. Perhaps it was Nomi, perhaps she's allowed only one call, should I not have waited, oh why did I not wait? I know all the while that the thought is preposterous, but the trembling does not stop until the caller, a friend from California, calls again, and this time can hear me.

That night, I cannot sleep. (And even now, as I recall the episode, I feel queasy. And even now, when, as sometimes happens, there's no reply to my "hello" on the phone, the thought crosses my mind: Nomi.)

But the magical explanations are no explanations at all, the fantasies are a fleeting self-indulgence. There was no trial, this is no punishment. Bad things happen to good people and good things happen to bad people; there is no dependable relationship between merit and reward.

No, my abiding "theology" is drawn from Camus and Sartre: Life is a series of accidents. The kids in Israel made that particular bus, the bus that would explode, and not another, by chance; their death was a random event. If Anne Frank hadn't contracted a trivial infection, she'd have been sent to a labor camp and might well have survived. And if my mother, or if my father, or if that car. . . . But with Nomi, the magical thinking aside, there are no "if only"s. If only she hadn't been where it happened when it happened, she'd have been in another, possibly a worse, place—alone with Liat at home, or in a car, or, a day earlier, on a plane from Florida. As it happened, CPR was started within seconds of her collapse, and the EMT was there right away, but both were already too late.

Not a few of the friends who came to visit and to pray during the traditional week of mourning observed that it is easier for those who believe, for those who know that God is always just, or who know that our loved ones are now with God, or, more generally, that there must be a reason, even if that reason is beyond our comprehension. Do I not envy the believers, they asked?

No, I do not. For me, a skeptic, there is here no crisis of faith; were I a believer, I cannot imagine being protected from such a crisis. Nomi with God? But Nomi belongs with Liat, and Liat, for sure, belongs with Nomi. There is a logic beyond comprehension? Then I cannot comprehend it, and it brings no comfort, and I cannot relate to its author.

Later, and for weeks, the letters of condolence will arrive. Many—fifty or more—will be from rabbis, men and women I've met in the course of my travels across the country. Not a single one will offer a theological handle, or even try to. Their modesty fits the mystery, the awful mystery of untimely death. Most will say instead, "I have no words to offer you." And then the ancient formula, "May you be comforted among the other

mourners of Zion and Jerusalem." Two go a gentle step farther: "In your unutterable loss, we, your friends, can bring
only our love and our hope. I cannot believe that Nomi is
extinguished. Somehow, somewhere, your grief must become
a part of the eternal." And, "There are times, someone said,
when God asks nothing of His creatures except silence,
patience, and tears. May your daughter's memory be a source
of consolation and open a door to peace in the face of turmoil
and pain." I am grateful to these two and to the others for their
humility and for their humanity. They pretend to no expertise
at that which cannot be fathomed; the comfort they propose
derives not from theology but from community, not from the
rational but from the ritual. That is, I believe, as it should be
when we are faced with impenetrable mystery. For me, it is as
it must be. Before that which cannot be penetrated, compre-
hended, explained, I rage, I weep, I resign, but I do not pretend to know what is on the other side of the wall or why my
daughter is there.

Back in the hospital, the chaplain apologized: "I have no
answers," she said. And I replied, "I have no questions." Not
"Why?" or "Why her?" or "Why me?" These are not questions,
they are cries of anguish. For surely there is nothing we know
by now with greater certainty than this: Every moment of
every day, the spinning wheel stops somewhere that it is not
supposed to, somewhere that makes no sense. Every moment
of every day, somewhere, a parent is bereaved, a child is
untimely orphaned, a dream dissolves. This time, the wheel
stopped here.

In their letters of condolence, two friends add touching
twists of their own: "May you be comforted in the dark places
where your own suffering is utterly unique, along with all the

mourners of Zion and Jerusalem in their own unique griefs."
And then, "May you and Nomi's family be comforted along with
all the mourners for the fractured Zion we seek to set aright."

At the end of the day on which we buried Nomi, I turn
to Sharon and say to her, "There wasn't a single hug that didn't
come as a comfort."

Nomi, alive

I miss her.

Once, when Nomi was about ten years old, I took her with me to New York. We flew down, took a cab to the brief meeting that was my excuse for the trip, and then went by subway to lower Manhattan, where we boarded a helicopter for an aerial tour of the city. I hadn't preplanned a day about modes of transportation, but once it became clear that we'd embarked on one, we became systematic about it—ferry to the Statue of Liberty, bus back to midtown, horse-and-buggy amble through Central Park. I think that covers it, but I am not certain, and I cannot ask Nomi whether I've remembered it all.

A past that is suddenly frozen. Or nearly so, since now and then I stumble across a forgotten detail. I look through a folder bulging with her papers—report cards, letters, school work, odds and ends—or a friend from one of the layers of her life volunteers a detail long since forgotten or perhaps never before known to me. "Do you remember," Mychal asks, "how many years it was between the time you promised to buy her a ring if she'd stop biting her nails and the day she showed you that all ten had grown out? You'd forgotten the promise, but she held you to it, and both of you were so proud when you gave her the ring." No, I hadn't remembered.

A long-since filed-away Father's Day card from Nomi: "Thanks for all you've done for me since last Father's Day— my trips to California, the new dresses, being there whenever I needed you. Your 'big shoulder' doesn't get any smaller from year to year. But most of all, the one thing I am grateful for more than anything else: Thanks, Dad, for teaching me how to wink!!" And I do remember, albeit vaguely—the kibbitzing, the scrunched-up face, the discussions of mind-over-eyelid.

But the reminiscence has the quality of one hand clapping. I miss her, miss being able to pick up the phone and say, "Guess what I just remembered," miss the quick hugs, miss her look of impatience when I wanted to take her picture. I feel lost, and cannot explain that. In conversation, when I refer to "my daughters," I feel as if I am betraying her, for I am already thinking "two" as I speak the words, the third is gone.

Soon there will be no more refreshed memories. Soon, there will only be what remains, and what remains will not be Nomi. It will be only my memory of Nomi, a memory likely to atrophy, to become more purely my very pale reconstruction of this person, no longer here to correct my errors and misimpressions. It is not mere memories I want to clasp tight, to love.

When she was accepted by the University of Chicago, I tried to lay back. Chicago is my alma mater, and I didn't want to press her into following in my footsteps. Alongside its brilliant academic reputation, the school was thought to be quite nerdy; in consequence, it was actually attended by a smaller fraction of the young people it accepted than any other major university. So the University of Chicago sent out recruiters to persuade the kids it had accepted to make it their choice.

One day, Nomi got a letter inviting her to a "demonstration class." The dean of students was coming to Boston, and would do a "typical" class on such-and-such a Sunday afternoon. Parents were invited, and I went with Nomi to the home of an alumnus where the class was to take place. I imagined we'd have a discussion of Vietnam, or of drugs, or of some other then-sexy topic; instead, we spent two and a half hours on a line-by-line analysis of a Dylan Thomas poem.

Nomi was utterly charmed, even smitten. She understood both the poem and the underlying message: The University of

Chicago is the kind of place that believes that if you spend a Sunday afternoon reading, really reading, one poem, you've used your time well. She chose Chicago, and I had a poster made of the poem. The poster has long since disappeared, as also the memory of what poem it was. I could, I suppose, write to the dean to find out. But what difference would it make?[1]

Years earlier—decades earlier, actually—I'd left for Chicago from the B&O railway station in Baltimore. My parents hadn't been enthusiastic about my leaving home, but the University of Chicago had seen fit to give me a full-tuition scholarship— tuition then was $230 a quarter, $690 a year—plus another $300 towards living expenses, and that made it no more expensive than staying in Baltimore and attending Johns Hopkins. My brother, eight years my senior, a Navy veteran and already a graduate student, persuaded my parents that it would be good for me to be on my own. (In fact, having just turned seventeen, I was too young to derive full benefit from the experience in Chicago. But I didn't know that until much, much later.) We stood on the train platform, I with my footlocker and duffle bag, my parents with their hesitations; we said our good-byes. Though none of us had ever been to Chicago, the notion that one of them might accompany me never entered our minds.

When Nomi's turn came, though she'd already been there to have a look, it was as wordlessly understood that either her mom or I would travel with her, help get her set- tled in her dorm. Most likely because it was my school she'd be attending, I, rather than her mom, was the designated escort. We'd sent her stuff out earlier—too much by far to

---

[1] This very morning, by nearly random coincidence, as I prepare to send the last pages of this manuscript to the publisher, I stumble onto and into the poem. It's Thomas's "Fern Hill," and knowing that does make a difference after all.

take with us on the plane—and, on the appointed day, flew off to Chicago. I'd promised myself not to impose my eyes on her, but I did want to show her around the neighborhood, share a few stories of the good old days. "Here was Stagg Field, where the secret work on the atomic bomb was carried on during the war, and here is where your mother and I had our first apartment, and this is the dorm where I lived, and over there is where Second City, the birthplace of improv theater, got started," all that after unpacking endless bags of sweaters and meeting her Indian roommate. And then, at Rockefeller Chapel, a convocation for new students and their parents.

"You'll have ample opportunity to discover your diversity," the dean of the College began. "I want to tell you what you have in common. What you have in common, quite obviously, is that you've all made the same idiosyncratic choice. You've chosen to come to this university. And I want to tell you how I understand that decision."

It was the fall of 1983. I'd sat in this chapel back in the 1950s when Nehru spoke there, and when the leading political columnist of the day, Walter Lippmann, spoke, and when I received my BA and then my MA. I'd attended neighborhood Thanksgiving services there, and once, the inauguration of a new president for the university.

And in this fall of 1983, the dean continued: "I understand your decision to mean that you are prepared, together with us, your faculty, to enter into a compact to resist 1984." And then he launched into a learned disquisition on freedom of inquiry. I was on the verge of tears, so proud was I of my alma mater's fealty to the best of the academic tradition, so proud that my daughter was, as I had been, taken so seriously. I leaned over, kissed her on the cheek, whispered, "You're in good hands, Skeeps," and was off.

Weaving a story

Out of the fragments, we weave our stories. Here is a Nomi story:

It begins in 1878. In that year, there was born in Poland a boy named Henryk Goldszmit. Goldszmit had an unhappy childhood, and, partly in response to that, he decided that when he came of age he would devote his life to making things better for kids in distress. And so he went to medical school and studied pediatric medicine, focusing not only on the physical health of young children but also on their education.

His most special interest was in the rearing of orphans, to whom he was drawn less by their need than by the fact that they were the perfect group on whom to test his remarkably innovative educational theories—he was a kind of precursor to John Dewey and progressive education, believing among other things that kids in orphanages should be self-governing from the age of three. He imagined, in fact, that one day he would lead a million youngsters educated according to his theories through the capitals of Europe in order to show people what could be accomplished if one did things the right way.

Early on, he began to write children's stories. These he wrote under a pen name, and it is by that name that he is today remembered by those who remember him. That name is Janusz Korczak.

In due course, Korczak became renowned throughout Poland, a kind of combination of Dr. Spock and Dr. Seuss. He wrote a regular column of medical advice in the Polish press and he had a weekly radio program on which he read his children's stories out loud. He was invited to read learned papers in Berlin, in New York, in Paris, in London. Indeed, to this day children in Poland read the stories of Janusz Korczak.

In 1939, when the Nazis took Poland, Korczak was the director of a Warsaw orphanage with nearly 200 Jewish children. When the Warsaw Ghetto was established, Korczak's friends offered to provide him with false identity papers so that he could remain outside its walls. He rejected their offer; he wanted the children to stay together. With them he moved to Chlodna Street, inside the ghetto.

He was by then a somewhat sickly man. We have his diary of those years, and it tells how with bandaged feet he would in the early hours of the morning hobble off to the cabarets and there beg a few zlotys from the winners at the gaming tables in order to buy black-market bread for his 200 children.

Until August 6, 1942 (three years to the day before Hiroshima), when the Nazis came for him and his children.

The reason that Dr. Janusz Korczak is remembered, the reason that UNICEF and Poland and Israel have all issued stamps in his honor and memory, has, alas, little or nothing to do with either his pedagogic theories or his children's stories. It has, instead, everything to do with the fact that we have eyewitness accounts of how, on that day, Dr. Janusz Korczak walked at the head of a column of 192 children, in one arm carrying the smallest of them and with his other hand leading a barely older one. He sang with the children along the way to the *Umschlagplatz,* and when he himself was offered permission to return home, he chose to stay with the children. With them he entered the trains, with them later that same day he met his death in Treblinka.

That is the beginning of the story. It continues in 1973, in a place called Auschwitz. There, I shared with the members of the United Jewish Appeal Young Leadership mission that I served as scholar-in-residence a poem by Nellie Sachs. Nellie Sachs, Nobel Laureate in Literature, 1966; Nellie Sachs, who had herself narrowly escaped the Nazi grasp. The poem is called "Chorus of Comforters," and its very first line seemed to me then to capture more poignantly than any I had ever read the terrible meaning of the Kingdom of Night, of the Holocaust. That line reads, "We are gardeners who have no flowers."

In the spring of 1974, I was in a place called Kiryat Shmoneh, a town in the north of Israel. There, the mayor asked whether I wanted to visit the school, by which he meant the school directly across the street from the apartment complex where a year earlier the PLO had killed nineteen Jews, nine of them children, students at that school. When you enter the lobby of the school and you turn to your right, you see a plaque with the names of the nine kids, and it tears your heart out that so many years later, new names of Jewish children are still being added to the list. And when you turn to your left in that school lobby, what you see is a portrait of Janusz Korczak, because it turns out that it is the Janusz Korczak Elementary School of Kiryat Shmoneh that you have entered.

Standing in that lobby that day, some six months after having been in Poland, haunted by the life and death of Korczak, haunted by the words of Nellie Sachs, I understood that Nellie Sachs, for all the hard beauty of her words, was wrong. Nearly 400 children come to the Janusz Korczak Elementary School of Kiryat Shmoneh every day to learn what it is to be a Jew and a human being and to learn those things with pride and with joy and with dignity. Those children are our flowers. As are, once we begin to think about it, the elderly in the homes our philanthropies support, and the poor people we seek to feed, and yes, our own children, too.

I write here as a Jew. Each people has its very own flowers, and then there are the flowers in the communal garden we share with all the other planters. As a Jew, I know not only that we have flowers in profusion, but that we are prodigious, even obsessive, planters. We plant not in the manner of innocents, skipping off to the fields there to scatter our seed. Our history has been too hurtful to allow such simple pleasures, hopes so naïve. No, we rise to plant knowing full well that that which we plant in the morning may well be trampled before night. But we are back the next morning. And the one after that. And the one after that. Because as much as we have known disappointment, we are prisoners of hope. We know not only what has been, but also what has been promised, and we will not let go the promise. For was it not written and were we not taught that "they who plant in sorrow will surely one day reap in joy"?

There, the story—not yet Nomi's—rested for a time. But in 1978, on the last day of Passover, it resumed, and began to become my daughter's. It was on that day that Nomi delivered the bat mitzvah talk about Isaiah that appears much earlier in these pages, the talk that tells how watching a television series on the Holocaust caused her to disbelieve Isaiah's prophecy of the wolf and the lamb lying down together. And it was only a few days later, on Holocaust Remembrance Day, that Nomi's teacher arranged for two Holocaust survivors to talk with her class at the Solomon Schechter Day School.

And the next day, as was and would remain her habit (a habit neither inherited from nor taught her by her parents), Nomi wrote them a letter of thanks:

Dear Mr. and Mrs. Natansohn:

In my *haftorah* portion, the recurrent topic is peace. 'And the wolf shall lie down with the lamb' is the main sentence of this *haftorah*. Because of this, and because the TV version of *Holocaust* had been aired just two weeks before my bat mitzvah, I chose the topic of faith to be the main topic of my bat mitzvah speech. My view of this issue was that after having just seen a reenactment of the most terrible event in Jewish history, I could not fully believe that the wolf shall lie down with the lamb and that peace will one day be here.

While listening to your speeches, the thing that amazed me most was your continuing faith in God. And it occurred to me that if people such as you, who have lived through such terrible conditions as you have, still have the faith and love left to believe not only in God, but in the goodness of people also, then people such as I, who have never had much reason to complain and be bitter, have much more reason to be grateful and have total faith in life.

So if I am ever called upon to give a talk about this *haftorah* again, my view will be different. Instead of not believing and not having faith, I will think of you and remember that I do not have the right not to trust and have *emunah* [faith], when around me people such as you have the right to complain and do not.

Thank you not only for coming in to share your dreadful experiences with us but also for opening my eyes and restoring my faith. Thank you for the transfusion of hope and belief you gave me.

That letter, written by a child not yet thirteen years old, became part of my own paraphernalia. I have carried it with me all these years, and have read it to considerable effect from lecture platforms across the country. (Nomi, knowing I was using her letter, would now and then chide me, asking for her fair share of my honorarium.)

Shortly after I first read Nomi's letter, with its arresting reference to the wolf and the lamb lying down together, there crossed my desk at *Moment,* a magazine I founded in 1975 and edited until 1987, a manuscript that, under normal circumstances, I'd have glanced at and tossed into the rejected pile. But because it was about a subject of some interest to me, I read it all the way through. The article was about the Janusz Korczak school in Kiryat Shmoneh. And there, on page six or so, I learned a fact that I'd had no reason to pay attention to back when I'd visited the school. To the outside wall of the Korczak school in Kiryat Shmoneh are affixed the words, *"V'gar z'ev im keves"*—"and the wolf shall lie down with the lamb."

And there, again, the story rested, become now a story of the marvelous intricacy of the Jewish tapestry.

The circles spread

And now I have come to understand that the story is one that never ends, its threads weaving around and into Nomi's life, and from that life into the lives of others.

After Nomi died, the headmaster of her school went through her student file and found there a letter addressed to her that had, by chance, been stuck in her file. It was still sealed, and she had never seen it. (I imagine it arrived after Nomi had graduated, and was simply placed in her file inadvertently.) The letter is from Sam Natansohn, the man to whom Nomi had written her letter of thanks. Here, in part, is what Mr. Natansohn, a survivor of the Holocaust, wrote to a then twelve-and-a-half-year-old girl:

Dear Naomi:

It is difficult to describe my feelings upon reading your letter. I was overcome by a sense of awe, humility and wonderment. I am awed by the impact that our words had on you; it is very rare that one human being can reach another one and evoke a reaction of this nature and magnitude. There may be nothing that I shall do for the rest of my life that could compare in significance to this event. I feel humble because I am not sure that I am equal to the task of inspiring such faith in you, that I deserve this particular *z'chut* [privilege, merit]. And I marvel at the way of the Lord who has rekindled your faith via a chance encounter. . . .

I can very well understand your despair about the future; it is understandable in view of all the cruel and senseless killings around us. But there are also some indications that may serve as augurs of the fulfillment of Isaiah's prophecy. Israel and Egypt just signed a peace treaty, as imperfect as it may be, and an Israeli ship just sailed through the Suez canal. The Catholic Church, our centuries' long enemy, has condescended to consider our religion as an acceptable expression of faith, removing the imperative of our conversion from their theology (although they still do not recognize Israel). A reasonably democratic election has been held in Rhodesia and there may yet be a peaceful solution to that seemingly impossibly complex problem. The United States and Communist China are not confronting each other in a hostile manner anymore. All these facts were unthinkable only a few years, even months, ago. So let us hope that, paraphrasing the words of your *haftorah*, the spirit of the Lord shall be resting upon all of us, the spirit of wisdom and understanding and knowledge, and in this manner we shall all be working towards the realization of Isaiah's vision, of eternal peace and amity among all.

I cannot thank you enough for your letter. It provided me with a rare moment of exultation in the great-
ness of the human spirit, something I believe in but have
little opportunity to witness. May God bless you in all
your endeavors.

My distress that Nomi never got to see the letter was bal-
anced by my awe in reading it. I was (and remain) astonished
that an aging Holocaust survivor, in writing to a not-yet thir-
teen-year-old, would think to cite a democratic election in
Rhodesia as grounds for hope in the human spirit. I felt
immense gratitude to Sam Natansohn, whom I had never
met, for what he wrote to my daughter, who never read his
words. And so, now that I had a name and an address, I
called—knowing, of course, that it was now eighteen years
since the letter had been written, that the odds this wise and
kind man would still be there, would still be alive, were not all
that good.

He was there, and his wife, Sidi, in a suburb not too far
from where I live, actually close by the cemetery where Nomi
is buried. I told them briefly how our lives had once intersect-
ed—they did not remember either Nomi's letter or their
reply—and we arranged to meet.

I brought the letters with me, read them aloud, thanked
them for the "transfusion of faith and hope" they once gave
my daughter, thanked them on my own behalf as well—for if
people who have lived through the Kingdom of Night can, as
the Natansohns have, rebuild their lives, raise up children,
have still the largeness of spirit to take the time to write, and
to write as they did, to a child they do not know, then, like
Nomi, I learn from them that we must never succumb to
despair, never permit the sorrows of the moment, no matter

how stabbing, to deter us from seeking to make Isaiah's words come alive.

And there, in the Natansohn's modest living room, still more threads of the story were revealed. In 1985, *Moment* magazine, of which I was still then the editor, published an article about YIVO, the center of Yiddish research in New York. A woman in Brooklyn saw that article and, on the strength of it, came to see YIVO's librarian, whom she had visited ten years earlier. Back then, she had sought advice: How might she preserve the scraps of paper on which her daughter, then seventeen years old, had smuggled her last letter to her mother out of a Nazi prison? The mother didn't want to discuss the contents of the letter; she merely sought advice. But now, ten years later, she asked for YIVO's help in translating the letter from Polish into English so that her grandchildren might read it.

The librarian complied, and then sent to *Moment* a copy of the translated letter along with her own letter explaining the circumstances by which it had come to her. We published both. In her letter, her last letter before being killed by the Nazis, the woman's daughter asks her mother to send her a cyanide pill so that she might put an end to her suffering.

How did a woman in Brooklyn come to see the article in *Moment* about YIVO? The answer is that she had a gift subscription that had been sent to her by her son, Sam Natansohn. The same good man who'd exchanged such remarkable letters with my daughter was the brother of the young woman whose letter I'd published. And I, who at that time did not know the names of the people to whom Nomi's letter had been addressed, had therefore missed the connection between the article we published and that letter.

Who can explain such intricate intertwinings? Who can comprehend the mysteries that weave one life into another, that take one story beyond its own boundaries and intermingle it with another story, and then another, and then another? Stephen Vincent Benet once wrote, "You drop a stone in a pond, and the circles spread. Who can ever say on what far shore of the pond the last circle will break?" He was right to ask the question, but wrong to think there is ever a "last circle."

This I have come to know in diverse ways, most recently by way of a letter from a man named Don Drumm, in Illinois, that reached me in the wake of an article I wrote about Nomi, an article in which I quoted her letter to the Natansohns. My article appeared in several Jewish newspapers around the country, and Drumm's was one response:

> Your words and Nomi's words touched my heart deeply. . . . They are words of wisdom, and I am now about to cut and paste your column with those wonderful words, yours and hers, and frame them, so that one day, not too far away, when my five-year-old daughter, Delia, and my four-year-old son, Byron, reach the age of 12, not yet 13, I will sit down with them and read them the wise Jewish story I will entitle, 'Naomi's Love for Humanity.'
>
> If I should cross the threshold before they reach that age (I am 58 at this writing) my children will discover this framed column in their Treasure Chest in the attic, and your heartfelt words and Nomi's words of wisdom will be passed on and live in the hearts of the next Christian generation.

Every life is a story; every life well lived is a story that never ends. Somewhere in Illinois, two young children, Delia and Byron, will (perhaps) live stories that are different from what they might have been because Nomi's story has become part of their own. In Illinois, and perhaps in a dozen or a hundred dozen other places we will never know about. That is how it is.

And if there are those who when I write "story" read "soul," I will not quarrel with their way of reading what I have written.

Nomi, dead

I believe every word I have written about the inadmissibility of despair. But alongside the belief, there is the persistent pain. Nomi's story is rich beyond measure, and it endures, even expands. But the Nomi we mourn was flesh and blood, with a horsy laugh and a penchant for watching soap operas; she was slender, lithe, and she carried her head a bit off to the side, as if always exploring. Her skin was too dry, and I delighted in buying elegant ointments to help soften it; she planned intricate surprise parties, loved letter writing, and hugged tight. She was a swept-away mother whom her daughter Liat will know only secondhand. Sermons, homilies, even wondrous stories cannot compensate for the hugs; they are entered in a very different ledger, a worthy ledger with many pages yet to be filled, but alongside that ledger there is another, entirely intimate, and on its last page it says, "Finished."

PART II

Meditations and Consolations

Encounters

TEN WEEKS HAVE PASSED SINCE THE DESOLATING DAY. THE SADness has deepened. I cry more frequently, the stories matter less. I reread what I wrote in a cathartic burst in the immediate aftermath, in the first few weeks, am reminded that I denied shock back then, but recognize now that I must have been in shock. I do not understand the fact of death, its absolute irreversibility. Everything we are taught indicates that verdicts can be appealed. If the house burns down, we build a new house; if we lose our job, we find a new job; if we fail the course, we take it again. But this? Again and again, I replay that Monday, the day she died: David's call, the drive to the hospital, the news. It does not change. The trial, the verdict, the sentence—one short breath and done. It is final: no mitigating circumstance, no clemency, no pardon, not then, not ever.

I walk across Central Park in New York, am suddenly alone, alone for the first time in more than three months—no phone, no friends, no computer or books to divert me. But I am not alone: The Angel of Death walks alongside me, reminding me, taunting me, and I cry my way across the park, from bench to bench.

I am at a playground with Rachel and Jessie—Liat's aunts, my daughters. I shoot a roll of film, help Liat down the slide. She kisses me. All of us sit on a bench for a bit. Jessie takes Liat by the hand and walks away from us, towards the springy horse. Out of nowhere, I begin to cry, say to Rachel, "It breaks my heart." Out of nowhere, indeed.

I attend Shabbat services. My friend, next to me, grabs hold of my hand and says, urgently, "Get ready. Rough time ahead." She's looked at the order of the service for the evening, knows that we've arrived at the song "The whole world is a very narrow bridge." She embraces me as I sob.

Six weeks after her death, Nomi's friends in Los Angeles arrange a memorial evening at Alonim, the summer camp she attended as a youngster, working her way up from camper to director of the counselor-in-training program. David, Jessie, Rob (then Jessie's fiance, now her husband) and I fly out to be there. We do it for her friends' sake, and for hers. We do it for ourselves as well; still immersed in our grief, it feels right to be with people who, unlike our friends at home, have not yet wept together, have not yet assimilated the fact of Nomi's death.

One night, Rashi and Ruth, my brother and his wife, stop by. I ask whether they have read anything that has brought them comfort, thinking that they have had nine months more than I to feel their way into this bereavement. I sense that my brother is tense; he begins to pace, and then he explodes: "I can't handle this; I don't want to be mean, but I cannot talk with you about these things. My scab is forming, and every time we talk you rip it off, and I start to hemorrhage."

What can I say in response? I must be silent, even though it means rendering this most strange connection between us useless, this connection that I'd supposed would offer a touch of much-needed strength.

I walk up Broadway, pass a Barnes & Noble bookstore, and there in the window is a display of a new book, *Letters From Motherless Daughters*. I hesitate, then enter the store, find the book. I browse its pages. As far as I can tell, none of the women here represented lost her mother so young; they all can recall the mother they lost. Liat? Still, many report that because they had no mothers during their own critical years, they do not know how to be mothers to their own children. Liat.

Indeed, I have discovered a whole literature by and for bereaved parents. Books arrive in the mail unexpected, sent by a thoughtful acquaintance or friend who wants to help console me. Here and there, as I browse through them, I find a phrase, perhaps even an idea, that offers some help. But in the end, I derive no comfort from this literature of grief and consolation. I set the books aside; perhaps it is simply too soon. I am not yet ready to translate and transform the experience, to cook it; it is still fresh, raw. The scab has not yet begun to form.

I am walking on Newbury Street in Boston and suddenly see my old friend Donald, whom I have not seen in many months. Donald, whose seven-year-old son was killed by a hit-and-run driver thirty years ago. At his son's graveside, I spoke, trembling. What does one say, what can one say, to parents who have lost a child? Now, so many years later, Donald and I embrace, our absurd new bond unspoken.

I am at Nomi's and David's house. Until now, the enameled sign on the front door read, "Nomi, David, and Liat," and each time I came to visit these last ten weeks, the sign stabbed at me, taunted me. Now David has changed the sign so that it carries only his family name. Nomi's name is gone, as now it must be. And each time I come to visit, it stabs at me, taunts me.

We are in the kitchen at David's house; I am singing to Liat. I begin with my favorite children's song, "I See the Moon and the Moon Sees Me," and catch myself. I do not want to sing these words of longing for "somebody I'd like to see." I begin a different song, and once again stop mid-sentence; how can I sing "Please don't take my sunshine away"?

Now Liat is asleep. David and I are back in the kitchen. We do not speak often, still less often of what is plainly on both our minds, in our hearts. But tonight is different. He wonders aloud: "Who will sing to Liat, who will be gentle with her? Nomi could do things I can't." I tell him about rereading my letters to Nomi, being thereby reassured that she knew how much I loved her. He responds, "And you know how much she loved you."

Nomi and David

When Nomi's pacemaker was being installed, we—Zelda and the girls and David and I—gathered at the hospital. The surgery took rather longer than expected, and we became somewhat apprehensive. Finally, a nurse came to the waiting room to update us. And asked to talk to David, Nomi's husband.

That was an interesting, somewhat disconcerting learning. Who is this David, and whence his priority? Was it he who changed her diaper, took her to Disneyland, helped her with her homework? Did he go to her recitals, watch her graduate from nursery school, from elementary school, from high school? Was it he who from the day she was born had been her assigned protector? None of the above. No, he is simply the man to whom she has pledged herself, the man to whom her most precious intimacies are now whispered, as nature and social convention have decreed. It is, in a way, an odd thing: A legal contract that may one day be dissolved (and often is), trumps, so long as it is in force, biology itself.

The contract that binds husband and wife is not, however, wholly a matter of law. I am David's father-in-law, Zelda his mother-in-law, but Nomi was not his "wife-in-law." She was his wife, his spouse, a relationship mediated and governed by law but rooted in the mysteries of love and commitment. When I toasted them at their wedding, I said (in part):

> As Nomi and David point out in their guidebook for this wedding, this is a double celebration. The community—the community of family and friends, and the larger community, too, the one whose representatives by virtue of the authority vested in them give legal weight to this proceeding—the community gathers formally to acknowledge its acceptance of and respect for the new boundaries that Nomi and David have chosen to draw, the new space they have chosen to create, their private space. Its acceptance, its respect, and its delight in their delight.
>
> The poet John Ciardi says that marriage is "most like an arch, two weaknesses that lean into a strength." With the world as it is, he writes, "what's strong and separate falters." Before they come together, all they do in "piling stone on stone" is "roofless around nothing." And then they kiss, and fall in on one another, and there's the arch. This new arch, Nomi and David's new strength, is one thing we gather to celebrate. The other celebration is for our own sake as much as for theirs, because we know that as they pile stone on stone and together build a new house, they add a new point of strength and beauty to our collective estate. On the door to their room, they are now fully entitled to hang a "do not disturb" sign, and

we are commanded to respect it, but there is no lock on that door, nor need for one: Theirs, to mix the metaphor, is a branch on a blossoming tree, and it draws its nourishment from staying connected to the trunk.

David, any man lucky enough to be loved by any of the three sisters would be fortunate indeed. All three have inherited the family tradition of caring and compassion, all three are wonderfully there for those who need them. You're the first, in the way that matters most, to have captured one of the three hearts, and the heart you've captured, and the mind that goes with it, are as rich and as lovely as any man could wish. I've known that all along, of course, but I know it better now, because the wisdom of her heart led Nomi to choose you, bringing still another blessing into my life. Nomi, I have, as I believe you know, very much to thank you for, and that's been true since you were a toddler. Most of all, I thank you for still believing that people are good at heart and for helping us, through your own heart's goodness, believe it, too. But today, I thank you for David. . . .

I knew all that, and believed it—but still, when the nurse asked to talk with David, I felt a pang. And again when Liat was being born: We gathered at the hospital, we visited with her briefly, and then left the room—all of us except David. And an hour that seemed more like a whole day later, it was David who emerged to bring us the glad news.

David

Yet I think both Nomi and I were terrific at the needed letting go, at creating the space to allow this new and embracing relationship to take its proper place in the center of Nomi's life. At letting go and staying, still, connected. On the one hand, we talked very nearly every day; on the other, there was a change in texture: Our talks were more for purposes of superficial update than for recapture of earlier intimacy.

That is why it pleases me more than perhaps it should to hear David speak now of Nomi's love for me, pleases me that her love remained intact, pleases me that he knows of it. It is not vanity but the fact that I will never again have the chance for a quiet walk with Nomi, a time for us to reflect on these things together, to talk about the tension between love and letting go. So David's words are a message from before the grave.

There's also this: Until now, my connection to David has been through Nomi, each of us accepting the other because both of us were loved by Nomi, each of us seeing the other principally through Nomi's eyes. Her eyes are now closed; now we must learn to see one another directly, without mediation. That will surely take many months, perhaps more. For now, each interaction is also an intrusion, forcing on us the awareness of how it was we came to be connected—and that she is gone. Still, that is where we begin, and the fact that David is aware of the bond between me and Nomi encourages my hope that we will work through this time, create and sustain our own bond. For Nomi's sake, for our own—and, above all, for Liat's.

David remains, of course, my son-in-law, and I have yet to think about such confusion as may be introduced into that relationship if and when he remarries. Plainly, we will stay "related," even if there is no term that accurately captures the relationship. (And what if he were not the father of my granddaughter? As I have since the early weeks come to realize, my relationship with David does remain largely mediated and in no small measure sustained by Liat.) Plainly, it is David whose world has been most transformed by the tragedy, he who has been most dislocated, he on whom the most tangible burden has now fallen. Yet one day, God willing, this chapter of his life—his life with Nomi, her death—will become for him exactly that: a chapter, followed by new and uplifting chapters that will stand on their own and render all this a bittersweet memory. And while no one will ever take Nomi's place, he will have, as all of us hope for his sake and for Liat's, a new wife, and Liat a new mother. (And I must hope that this new person will at least not mind the presence in Liat's life of Nomi's family.) Liat will become, as she should, more a link to the future than to the past. And he will love his wife fully.

The arithmetic of death is not constant. We, the original and nuclear family—our composition has been forever diminished, the nucleus invaded. We were five, and now we are four; the absence can never be changed. No, that gives us no priority as mourners. It is just there, one of those tiny facts that now and then bob into view. The company of the bereaved is a company connected by memory and loss—but in the end, each member of that company experiences both memory and loss uniquely, alone.

A question

What's a father for?

A father is to protect his child. Does this mean that when the child dies, the father has failed? But the protection that is his assignment is not only against the things that go bump in the night or strangle the heart in the day. Eventually, we die; against that destiny, there is no protection. The only safety we can assure our child is the safety that comes of being loved, well and wisely. But love is not a protection against death; it is a shelter within life. Our challenge is not, cannot ever be, death's defeat; it is, it must be, life's opportunities. Among these, the challenge of love, of its giving and of its receiving, is primary.

When we feed a child, and hug a child, and teach a child, we are not blocking death's door; we are opening the door to life, to life as a sacred gift.

A sacred gift? Is that not our vanity speaking? How can this spark so soon extinguished be taken seriously? For even if we live to an old age so ripe that we fall gently from the tree of life, we have lived but an instant in the sweep of time. Ten years, thirty years, a hundred years—so what? This morning's paper reports that the sun will die in five billion years, our Earth some time before that. Is not everything then an illusion?

But this is what we have, what there is. The question is not whether life is merely an accident; of course it is. The question is whether we have the will to impose meaning on the accident of life, of our lives.

Context

Most often, death is an unremarkable fact of life. In due course, people die: "In the fullness of time." Sad, but hardly tragic. Sometimes I wonder whether we'd feel differently if there'd been some familiar context to Nomi's death—a disease, an accident, some such. The utter suddenness adds, I think, to the incomprehensibility of what happened. And that incomprehensibility, in the end, is among the most distressing and enduring aspects of the tragedy. Over and over again, I review the events of that day. Over and over again, I come up hard against an impenetrable wall. There is no way around that wall, no way to tunnel under it or climb over it, and it stretches endlessly.

No, I do not feel that way about my mother and father. They were buried at the end of life's path, and though I cannot walk that path, they are where they are supposed to be. Not so Nomi. Not so Bena.

The only context is the vague historical context: Sometimes people die out of order. Nor is the history of unnatural death just an ancient text. This year, some millions of children will die of hunger and disease, or by stepping on land mines left over from war's madness. Here in the West, there are some (many?) who imagine—if they pause to think of such things at all—that death is so common in those parts of the world where hunger prevails that parents there are less affected by it than we here are. Nonsense. Grief is an entirely universal language.

But grief is not our only universal language. Once, some years ago, I was in Egypt, in one of those Cairene cemeteries where poor people make their homes. There I saw a family— father, mother, a daughter who was perhaps seven—busy building a hut. They were building it of mud: The little girl scooped mud into a bucket, the mother carried the bucket up a ladder, and there, on the roof, the father applied the mud. They saw me, and the father climbed down. With great pride he showed me the hut. We had no language in common, but none was needed.

I clucked admiringly and, after a short while, began to leave. But after just a few steps, I stopped and turned back, holding out two twenty-dollar bills to the father—for him, the equivalent of three or four months' wages. With evident pride, he said *"La,"* one of the few Arabic words I know: "No." I sought to press the money on him; he wouldn't take it. Not, that is, until I looked over at his daughter, pointed, and said, "It's for her. I have daughters of my own."

It was not my words, spoken in a language he did not understand, that caused him finally to take the money. It was my gesture towards his daughter; that he understood, and his pride gave way to his love.

On my part, no more than a gesture. On his, no less a concern and commitment to a child than the rest of us. How very arrogant and insular to think otherwise. Not only grief, but a parent's love, is a universal language.

I do not think these are just "pretty words." Neither, however, are they an adequate offset to my sense of failure. Love is crucial, and once, in a sweet and memorable way, the language of love—the love of children—became my means of communicating with another father. Nice, really nice. So what? Do I now search out such memories in order to prove to myself that Nomi did not die on account of my failings? (And, in any case, do occasional grace notes such as this drown out those failings?) I am not in the grip of a neurotic delusion. I know that there was no way at all I could have prevented what happened. I know that rationally, and I know that emotionally. Perhaps, therefore, what I have now learned is something I should have known more powerfully all along: A father is only a father, a parent only a parent. You cannot (and would not want to) fashion a cocoon for your child, you cannot supervise happenstance; no matter how many strings you gather in your hands your child is not your puppet, not even when she is a small child, surely not when she has become a woman.

Tension

When thirty days have passed, as custom prescribes, we gather with family and friends for a service. The form of the service is open; we have chosen, more or less, to study together. Josh Elkin walks us through a section of the Talmud; I tell a long Nomi story, the story that begins with Janusz Korczak that I told earlier in these pages. And my dear friend, Rabbi Rachel Cowan, teaches a psalm. The psalm she has chosen is number forty-two:

> *Like a hind crying for water, my soul cries out*
> *for You, O God;*
> *my soul thirsts for God, the living God;*
> *O when will I come to appear before God?*
> *My tears have been my food day and night;*
> *I am ever taunted with, "Where is your God?"*
> *When I think of this, I pour out my soul:*
> *how I walked with the crowd, moved with them,*
> *the festive crowd,*
> *to the House of God with joyous shouts of praise.*
> *Why so downcast, my soul, why disquieted within me?*
> *Have hope in God; I will yet praise Him for His*
> *saving presence.*
>
> *O my God, my soul is downcast; therefore I think*
> *of You in this*
> *land of Jordan and Hermon, in Mount Mizar,*
> *where deep calls to deep*
> *in the roar of Your cataracts;*
> *all your breakers and billows have swept over me.*
> *By day may the Lord vouchsafe His faithful care,*
> *so that at night a*
> *song to Him may be with me, a prayer to the God*
> *of my life.*

I say to God, my rock, "Why have you forgotten me,
why must I walk in gloom, oppressed by my
*   enemy?"*
Crushing my bones, my foes revile me,
taunting me always with, "Where is your God?"
Why so downcast, my soul, why disquieted
*   within me?*

Have hope in God; I will yet praise him,
my ever-present help, my God.

And she talks and wonders with us, gently, about the never-ending tension between hope and despair.

Different tracks

No, I do not cry all the time. I laugh, and I work, and in the morning, it is sometimes as much as thirty minutes before I remember that I have awakened to a life without Nomi— without, that is, the living and loving Nomi. For it is wrong, of course, to say that this is a life without Nomi. It is, in fact, at least so far, a life more filled with Nomi than ever. The presence of her absence is haunting; the presence of her irreversible absence.

It is as if I live now on three distinct tracks. One is the track of loss and of grief. Another is the track of work, of play, of life as it was. Often, these two tracks intersect. Every day, in the midst of the work and the play, there come reminders of the loss. Often, they come from the outside—a belated condolence letter or call, a visit with Liat, a song Nomi loved, a sappy television commercial, the wail of an ambulance siren. Often, I am asked how many children I have. I hesitate: I cannot say "two," that would be a betrayal. Yet if I say "three," the next question is typically, "And where are they?" So I pre-empt the question, volunteer that one died. (Not "is dead." "Died" refers to an event, "is dead" to a condition, and the event is somehow less painful than the condition.) And often, the reminders simply come; nothing special is needed to trigger them.

Then there is a third track: Like the track of loss, with which it does not intersect, it is new to me. Like the track of life, with which it must come to intersect in ways I cannot yet understand, it leads to places unknown. It is the track of community—of love and thoughtfulness, of a holy and healing reaching out that has meant so very much these past few months. It does not, it cannot, change the fact of Nomi's death; it does—more accurately, it will, I think—change the facts of my life, though I cannot yet say how. The tear of my suit, the break in my life: There was before, and there is now after. After, I must be more circumspect; there are dangers I cannot defend against, obstacles I cannot overcome. Thus aware of my own shortcomings, I must be more accepting of others' lapses and deficiencies. And after, knowing how deeply I was touched and how powerfully protected by others' kindness, I must listen better—listen to their stories, to their needs, to what they can teach me.

Letters

From a letter, we learn that on the day of the funeral, Nomi's friends in Jerusalem gathered to remember her. Nomi's friends, including Debbie, who will later tell me how she resented Nomi when she first met her. She'd had a date with David, liked him, hoped he'd call—but weeks later, he still hadn't. Then she went to a party, and when she arrived she saw him—and Nomi was sitting on his lap. A mutual friend told her that Nomi and David had just "officially" crossed over the line from being "friends" to being "boyfriend/girlfriend." Debbie's jealousy, she told me, "lasted about seven minutes. They were obviously meant to be together. And Nomi, as beautiful a person as she was, was not someone to be jealous of. When she died, I felt as if a big chunk of my happiness died too. And the world lost one of the people who brought happiness to it."

Another letter recalls for me a phrase Mychal used in her eulogy for Nomi, when she referred to Nomi as "a kids' kid and an adults' kid." The letter is from Bonnie Hausman, a casual acquaintance from years ago:

> I barely knew Nomi as an adult. I knew her best as Nomi, a bouncy, happy seventh/eighth grader at Schechter. There, when I would pick up or deliver my 1st grader (Tamara, now 24), I would have occasion to observe and frequently interact with Nomi. Or, I should say, she would make it a point to interact with me.
>
> "Hi, Mrs. Hausman, how are you," she would say, stopping in the hall to greet me, knowing that I had some connection to her family from somewhere, sometime. She was very rare. How many seventh/eighth graders interrupt their exchange with their peers as they move through the school corridors to greet a grown-up they barely know? Only Nomi Fein. I quickly decided that this is the way all children should be—at least, this is the standard I would set for my own.

And from my friends at Brandeis University: "There is a certain quiet mood here today. So many of us here know what happened, shake our heads in disbelief and upset, and then there is a general collective silent cry for what has taken place."

I quote from these letters and from others because my own experience has taught me that we—at least some of us—are often inhibited in the face of another's tragedy, feel that our words are so inadequate that we remain silent. And it is true that our words cannot change the tragic fact that is their occasion. But that is not their function. Their function is only to provide comfort. And yes, they do comfort. I cannot say precisely why. Because I am not, after all, entirely alone? Because misery loves company? Because it is flattering that people care?

But why must I answer the question? Here I am, in pain, and these letters are a balm. That is enough. "I hope your deep creative resources will prove a strength in this astonishing ordeal. Words seem so paltry, but how else to let you know my prayers are with you?" It is the word "astonishing" that touches me; how does the writer know how utterly astonishing this is in its bleakness? "I don't know what to write, but I want you to know that my heart is breaking for you." And so on.

Mostly, the letters are from people I know, though many of those who write are from barely remembered chapters of my past. Some are from strangers. Often, the wording is clumsy. Yet I look forward to the stuffed mailbox, experience withdrawal pangs when the letters taper off. Again, the question: What is it about all of them that touches me so deeply?

Sometimes, of course, it is what people choose to write. Invariably, those who knew Nomi have something sweet to say about her, and their words are especially touching. But most did not know her. They write instead of their shock, of their concern for me. During those first weeks, those weeks when it would have been so easy to shut the world out, or to curse it, the volume of letters was a daily announcement that there is kindness, generosity in the world, that people, even when they do not know what to write, insist on making their presence known, presuming—correctly—that even the simplest announcement of that presence will come as a comfort. The letters paper over the emptiness.

Again and again, the letters in fact begin with, "I don't know what to write." No matter. It is the fact of reaching out rather than the content that registers. Even the store-bought prewritten cards, on the whole a tacky choice, make a difference. (But spare me, please, the typed letters that conclude with the secretary's initials. Almost always, these offer such formulaic consolation that I suppose they are pulled from a drawer of "Forms For All Occasions." And spare me also the typed letters with multiple signatures, resembling petitions more than expressions of genuine concern and regard. But: Having promised myself to be less judgmental, why do I now violate that promise?) The people—there are many—who have taken the time to write, to reflect, to find a phrase or a poem, to share an insight, even the people who blurt out that "yours is the most terrible loss a person can know"—a fact of which I scarcely need to be reminded—are meaningful beyond measure. (But yes, then it occurs to me, as if this is Comparative Grief 101—is not Liat's loss still more terrible?)

I confess it: In my head, I carry a list, a short list, of the people who should have written (or called) and did not. As—this is the more painful confession—my name appears on other people's similar lists. We are, almost all of us, awkward around the fact of death, rendered either speechless or banal.

It is easier not to write, not to visit, and I have done my share of not writing and not visiting. No more. The wisdom of the ritual forms of comfort and of the etiquette of condolence cannot be exaggerated. Even the belated expression of sympathy is better, far better, than silence.

Gifts to the bereaved

People say things in these letters that I find surprising—kind things, gracious things, acknowledgments of what I have meant to them or to others. What they write along these lines is pleasing, but it does not correspond to my perception of myself. Some of what they write I discount; the occasion induces sentimental exaggeration. Words like "love" are used with uncommon, undisciplined, abandon. And what's true of a "normal" death is here, because of the shock, because the nightmare of a child's death has surely terrified my correspondents, still more inflated. But the content of the hyperbole is so uniform that I am given pause by it. Can it be that I have deserved such expression? I, who have perceived myself as (at best) only middlingly available to others? Can it be that these expressions of warmth, of a warmth that goes well beyond regard, are genuinely intended?

Oddly, I find myself addressing the "what have I done to deserve this" question not to the tragedy that has befallen me, but to the embrace that has been proffered me. "Please know," a very distant acquaintance writes, "that our entire family and extended community, all people who have been deeply touched by you and your family, stand with you in this time of inexplicable loss and pain. Feel our touch as we have felt yours." What is it, when was it, I try to remember, that I did for them? I do not recall. Yet, though puzzled, I feel their touch.

It is not just the letters, although I can scarcely exaggerate how much solace they provided during the weeks in which they flooded in. (At first, I'd call Jessie to read her the most touching letters. But she was in a different place. Nomi was her best friend, with whom she spoke four or five times a day, and the kindness of strangers could not penetrate her sorrow.) In addition to the letters, there have been calls; there were the people around the country who got word to me that at their Sabbath services following Nomi's death, mention was made of what had happened, she was included in the list of those for whom the kaddish prayer was that week recited; there were the people who made special trips to Boston during the week of *shiva*, mourning, to spend a few hours with me. (And among these were two who avoided the opening question that almost all others asked, the entirely unanswerable question, "How are you doing?" and said instead, ever so gently, "Tell me about your daughter." An invitation that opened the floodgates, and gave me permission to relieve the pressure building up behind the wall of conventional inhibition. I told them, I'm certain, much, much more than they'd bargained for—but I sensed that the point of their question was less to learn about Nomi than, insightfully, to allow me to talk, and talk.) On the Saturday following Nomi's death—the rites of mourning are set aside on the Shabbat—a dozen or so people I'd invited came to visit, and I told Nomi stories.

But now, before these expressions fade from memory, I must figure out what to do with them: where to put them, how to build on—and deserve—the kindness they represent. A friend with whom I shared many of the letters, and also my reaction to them, observed, "In some ways, you are listening to your own eulogy." There is some truth in that, as if the circumstances lead people to say only the nice things there are to say. But now that I have been granted a glimpse into a future I will not experience, I am challenged to live up to the appraisal. And the challenge is worth taking up even if all the good words were meant as gifts to a bereaved father rather than as serious assessments.

For now, all I know for sure is this: Nomi's untimely death shows that one may never take anything for granted, not even the most (until now) axiomatic sequence of the generations. But if one may not take such basic expectations for granted, why take for granted the gift of people's thoughtfulness, their kindness?

The kindness, and wisdom, of a stranger

A letter arrives from Oklahoma, written by a rabbi I have never met. He has read the same article that prompted Don Drumm's letter. He writes that my column reminded him of the immortal rabbinic dictum *g'villin nisrafin v'ha'otiot porchot ba'avir* ("the parchments are burning, and the letters blossom in the air.")

This, from a stranger. Normally, I am a tad resentful when someone begins a citation by informing me it is "well-known" or "immortal." Often—and if from the Talmud, very often—I do not know it. But here I am like a little child, open to and grateful for instruction.

I reflect on the words "the parchments are burning, and the letters blossom in the air." Their origin, I learn, is in the Talmud, where we are told that when Rabbi Hanina ben

Taradion was martyred by the Romans, they "wrapped him in the Scroll of the Law, placed bundles of branches round him, and set them on fire. They then brought tufts of wool, which they had soaked in water, and placed them over his heart so that he should not expire quickly." And when his disciples called to him, "Rabbi, what seest thou?" he answered, "The parchments are burning but the letters are soaring on high."

The word for "soaring" is also the word for "blossoming," and I have chosen the latter. It is interesting, I think, that it is the letters, rather than the words or the sentences or the paragraphs, that have been set free from their places in the parchment, have been deconstructed. For that leaves us with letters to be reconnected, reconstructed, fashioned into words, the words into sentences, the sentences into paragraphs, the paragraphs into stories that make sense to us. Once the letters have been let loose from the parchment, they may, it seems, be combined in endless ways; there is more than one story. So the new stories will never mirror the old, even though they will partake of them.

The story of Nomi that I have been telling is not the same story that others would tell, do tell, surely not the story that Nomi would have told had she had the chance; it is *my* story of Nomi, and it is therefore about what I remember, about how I see things and how I tell the things I see, about my Nomi. It is a true story, but so, too, are all the others. That is the blossoming.

The first Passover

Passover is approaching, just ten weeks after the fateful fatal day. I prepare the music we will sing together at the seder table. Among our favorite songs is *Al Kol Eleh,* whose words translate from the Hebrew: "Watch over all of these for me, good God—the honey and the thorn, the bitter and the sweet, our infant daughter. . . . Do not uproot that which has been planted . . ." The song derives from a very different context, but we dare not sing these words this year, or perhaps ever again. And once again, by now every day, the tears.

The seder: Five of Nomi's friends are here, have come as much to commemorate Nomi and to comfort her family as to celebrate this festival of freedom. David's family is here, too, as are Rashi and Ruth along with the usual guests at my Passover table. I am determined not to allow Nomi's absence, and Bena's, too, to overwhelm the ancient ceremony that is so central to my yearly calendar. I begin, therefore, with a riff on not taking things for granted and on our gratitude for what has been given to us, including the Passover seder we are about to begin, our people's passage from slavery to freedom, and the wisdom of our sages in crafting so elaborate and timeless a ceremony to commemorate that freedom. We must be grateful for all these things—and if there's pain that mingles with our gratitude and sometimes even overtakes it, we know that the *maror,* the bitter herbs, are also part of what we have been given.

Words are so often, perhaps too often, my preferred salve, my refuge, a way of transforming raw feelings into comforting abstractions. And there's a danger in that. Elie Wiesel once wrote, "Words name things, and then replace the things they name." I am fully aware of the degree to which I here use words to muffle the reality, to replace the thing itself. Now and then, as I wait for sleep, I set the words aside, look with my mind's eye directly at death, at Nomi's death. More often, I force my thoughts in some other direction, lest sleep become impossible. But when fully awake, I stand aside, letting the words take over. That is a writer's gift and curse.

This seder night, words offer only the most superficial protection. Ten weeks ago, Nomi was brilliantly alive; tonight, no words can soften her absence. Everyone at the table is committed to the ritual, indeed eager to become lost in its familiarity. But tonight the traditional question, "How is this night different from all other nights?" is double-edged: How indeed? Here are the friends, a tad too determined to ensure that celebration defeats sorrow; here is David, too young by decades to be a widower; here is Liat, a motherless child.

Liat is not the only motherless child at our table tonight. My friends Havi and Andy have come, and with them Andy's daughter, Tali, a high school senior. When Tali was just four, she and her mother, Anita, were vacationing at Ras Burka in the Sinai Desert. A berserk Egyptian policeman began to shoot at the tourists; Anita, wounded, threw her body over Tali's to protect her. The mad Egyptian threatened to shoot anyone who approached; Anita bled to death.

Tali is a delight—bright, charming, lively. I know, I know for a fact, that we can take nothing for granted—but oh! how I want to believe in the resilience of motherless children.

Death's warmth

I wonder, sometimes, whether there may not be some way to extend into ordinary time the warmth that the drama of death evokes. (And is it not strange to write of "warmth" in connection with death, which we commonly think of as terrifyingly cold?) The embrace, real and metaphoric, is so rich, so affirming and sustaining. Must we hold it in reserve, call it up only in the wake of tragedy, remain the rest of the time inhibited? I've wondered about that before, in the wake of floods and fires and little girls falling into abandoned mine shafts and volunteers from around the country then converging in a cascade of kindness. The likely answer, I'm inclined to think, it that the emotions that are accessible to us in the wake of death and disaster are, in fact, unique. It makes sense, however regrettable, that we cannot live daily at the high pitch that tragedy enables, encourages.

Still, to say that death stands alone, that we know intuitively that our capacity for kindness is an antidote of sorts to death, is not to say that what we learn of ourselves and our capacities in moments of ultimate drama has no application at all in more mundane times. In the wake of death, our conventional protections collapse, our vulnerability is exposed. Perhaps, once the active mourning is done, once we've glimpsed the kindness, learned that at least among our friends our vulnerability is accepted, even respected, we can be less guarded. I dare not forget how much I welcomed the hugs on the day we buried Nomi. I do not want to forget that I am capable not only of hugging but also of allowing myself to be hugged.

Given who Nomi was, what she was about, it would be easy to say that all this is a way of honoring her memory. I do not see it that way. Nomi is no more an icon dead than she was alive. But if the fact of her death has enabled us to learn something of ourselves—oh, how costly a lesson!—then we would be stupid to cast aside that learning or to let it atrophy.

At the same time, I know that new lessons, for all the sense of revelation that they may evoke, tend to fade rather quickly, unless one works to keep them alive, to sustain them until they become habit. Perhaps that is one reason I write this book: my effort to internalize what I sense I have learned. I do not want the learning to be wasted. And I want, for whatever these words may be worth to others who are bereaved, to others who seek to offer comfort, to write them in a manner that will enable others to read them.

Community

Nomi and David belonged to a congregation called the Newton Centre Minyan. (The word *minyan* refers to the quorum required for the recitation of certain prayers. More generally, as in this instance, it suggests a close-knit community.) David still belongs, and on most Sabbaths, he and Liat are there, in the local church where the Minyan meets. The Minyan, which numbers some 130 families, includes a fair number of Brandeis professors and other scholars. When Nomi and David moved to Newton, they "shopped" around for a bit, settled on the Minyan because it included a number of young couples, because its worship services suited them, and because its service is both traditional and wholly egalitarian, offering women full participation in every aspect.

Word of such a death as Nomi's spreads swiftly, mysteriously; the first member of the Minyan showed up at the hospital scarcely an hour after the futile effort to revive her was abandoned. From that moment on, the Minyan was a hovering, nurturing presence. For the seven days of mourning and the Shabbat they surrounded, it was members of the Minyan who prepared and brought and set out the food. When it snowed, it was they who shoveled the walk. And it was they who came to Nomi and David's house, morning and evening, to pray.

Often, there is concern in a house of mourning that there will not be the ten people that are required by Jewish tradition for the prayer service. At Nomi and David's, there were never fewer than forty people for the morning service—at seven o'clock, night's darkness just beginning to lift—and twice that or more, crowded into the small house, for the evening service.

David knew some of the Minyan members who surrounded us, embraced us, sustained us, but most he had not yet met. These were not, in the main, among the friends of one or another member of the family (who also came in number). They were simply members of the community that Nomi and David had joined, and it is a community that takes itself—its devotions, its commitments—seriously. And so, flawlessly, it rose to the sorry occasion. On the Friday afternoon of the *shiva* week, I watched in wonder as a virtual caravan of cars delivered food for the Shabbat meals—Friday dinner, Saturday lunch and dinner—for the fifteen or so family members who'd be together. Finally, I said to one of the drivers, "I hope that you don't do this only for tragedies." He smiled, and said, proudly, "You should see the way we do a baby-naming." (But of course a baby-naming is a one-shot occasion. Months later, the Minyan was still delivering the Sabbath meal for David and Liat. Still, perhaps here is one answer to the question of how we extend the kindness born of tragedy into ordinary time: The community of those who offer comfort is strengthened by its action, and the invigorated community becomes still more energetically an agent of kindness.)

I've been reading about "the loss of community in America" for just about as far back as I can remember. (David Riesman was my teacher at the University of Chicago the year his classic *The Lonely Crowd* was published. Why, oh why, did I cut so many classes?) That there's been such a loss is plainly the "sociologically correct" assumption. But now and then, I've wondered whether it is quite as pervasive as the analysts and essayists say. Might it not be, instead, that analysts and essayists (I among them), dealing as we do in abstractions, are ourselves often less rooted in neighborhood, workplace, church, that the "loss of community" reflects our own projected yearning rather than the more conventional American reality? Perhaps, then, the Newton Centre Minyan is not so remarkable, so unusual. But, whatever the sociological truth, the Minyan is new to me, and stunning in its devotion, in its generosity—the more so since so many of its members are analysts, essayists, and kindred folk.

Rules of grieving

There's a new book out, a compilation of memoirs by parents who've lost a child. The review I read the other day—I don't yet know whether I'll read the book—says that many of the parents are so marked by the experience that their bereavement consumes them, takes over their lives. (It says also that the acute grief lasts, typically, from four to six years.) Am I, then, atypical? I go to meetings and sometimes an hour or more passes before I remember. I watch a basketball game, read a book, buy groceries, and am, for a time, not conscious of my bereavement. I know already that the day will come, whether soon or late, when the awareness of loss will have drifted into the background, receding not for an hour or more but for long stretches of time. I know such a day will come, but I cannot yet imagine it. And I am certain that when it does come, "long stretches of time" will mean no more than a morning, an afternoon. Never a whole day without the sudden sharp awareness.

I have known all along that there are no rules, no norms, for grieving. We move, as we must, each of us in our own way. I write these pages, and, while I am writing, Nomi is both nearer to me and farther from me. She stands looking over my shoulder at what I am writing, but because she now comes alive only through the courtesy of a computer chip, and because this vivid person is here reduced to words on a screen, I am putting her away. She is in a distant room I cannot enter.

We must make space for one another's ways of grieving. People call and ask, "How are you doing?" What shall I, what can I say? "So so" seems the safest answer, whether I have been sobbing a moment earlier or been far from grief. If I say, as sometimes I feel, "terrific," will they not think me insensitive? If I say, as sometimes I feel, "wretched," what burden am I placing on them? (By now, I have developed an "okay" spoken in just the right tone, a way of communicating that I'm not exactly okay at all, but that I'm coping.) And how long will it be before I do not hear in their question the unspoken concern, before they do not intend by their question more than a perfunctory greeting?

There are, thank God, a handful of friends to whom I can sometimes say how I truly feel, although even with them I am often reluctant to be entirely open, fearing that I will be imposing on them. For what can they say, and what can they do? In the end, the harsh fact, immutable, remains.

Names

In Israel, at least until recently, a bereaved father would some-times change his name, calling himself father-of-[the name of the son who has died.] (So far as I know, it is only fathers who did this, and only sons for whom they did it.) I have no such disposition, not at all. I want to continue to be who I was before, as best I can be. Diminished, of course, by this terrible loss; perhaps also enlarged by the lessons that come in its wake. I am not "Nomi's Father." I am a man whom misfortune has visited, but who will not be wholly defined by that mis-fortune. As to names, the only name change I desire, and that only sometimes and only vaguely, is Liat's; I hope that to her middle name, "Gabrielle," can be added "Fein," so that she will carry with her the consciousness of our family, no matter what. Soon I may find a way to suggest this to David. Or per-haps my need will pass.

Some day, not long from now, God-willing, a new child will be born into this family, and if it's a girl, chances are it will be named in accordance with the tradition: Naomi. My tears these many months have come in bursts, quick thunderstorms that rage and then cease. But when her namesake arrives, I'd best be alone, for I will want to weep, and weep. How very hard it will be.

How lovely, how right, but how very hard.

Bena

A day we have been dreading approaches, the day of the unveiling of my niece Bena's stone.

Bena and Nomi, Nomi and Bena: Not close in life but now irrevocably connected. During Bena's last weeks, we'd all been drawn in, as families will be, by her crisis. Yet for all its gravity, I do not think we faced the awful possibility of Bena's death. We odds-beaters, we winners—even after the bone marrow transplant, during the twenty-eight days of the countdown to stem cell renewal, the days of wrapping ourselves in sterile masks and gowns and shoe coverings before entering her room—death remained remote, beyond the boundary of our active consciousness. Until something went wrong, and the threat could no longer be denied.

I'd thought of myself as an indifferent uncle, cordial but hardly intimate. But much as the aftermath of death encourages kindness, so does death's frequent prologue, life-threatening illness, beget intimacy. I was drawn to the hospital day after day, drawn by my own need as also my brother's. Rashi is perceived, and with good reason, as super-rational, a man whose thoughts are expressed in numbered order, whose most obvious passions are principally intellectual, and whose private sentiments are rarely displayed. Different though we are in personal style, and difficult as it may be to claim friendship with one so guarded, we are, indeed, quite close, much closer than most male siblings I know. Above all, and notwithstanding the reservations he's had about various choices I've made over the years, he has always—always—been available to me. And there was, at least for that unarticulated reason, no question that I must be available to him, as best I could, now. And once, as we walked near the hospital on a day that hope verged on collapse, he wept, and I was pleased, even flattered that he was able to. As I was when I was asked to join the nuclear family at what proved to be the surreal final conference with the doctors.

We'd known since the early morning that this would be the day, the end. Bena's kidneys had failed the night before, her other organs begun to shut down. Nature had defeated science, preempted human intervention. Yet as if insistent on the appearance of control, the doctors scheduled a meeting with the family for late in the afternoon.

The young physician who was charged with putting the matter on the table tried to soften his presentation by saying, "She's not doing as well as we'd hoped." As well? Down the hall, Bena was dying, alive still only by virtue of machines. But "not doing as well" implied she wasn't doing all that badly.

It was Karen, blunt Karen, Bena's sister, who refused to let the remark pass, and forced candor onto the table. And soon after, it was Rashi who spoke for the family, asking only that we be given time for each of us to say good-bye. And two days later, it fell to me to offer a eulogy for Bena.

Only now, reflecting on the event, did it occur to me to call up the words of that eulogy to the screen, and only now, therefore, have I understood how much working through what I could say to a grieving family then helped prepare me for my own still more immediate encounter with grief nine months later:

How do you summarize a life unfinished, a life so rudely and untimely interrupted?

How do you console a family so rudely and unjustly diminished? And how do you make sense out of, or even simply comprehend, so senseless, so cruelly random, so utterly incomprehensible an event?

How do you summarize Bena's life? Look around. Those here assembled, come together to say good-bye to her today, come as friends old and new from nearly all the many different precincts of her life, come as family old and young from Boston and Washington and

Baltimore and Trenton and Albany, from Florida and Los Angeles and San Francisco and Palo Alto, from Israel, from a dozen other places—we here, added together as we are today, are the living summary.

I mean that not just as rhetoric; I mean it quite literally, precisely. For each of us here carries not only memories of Bena; each of us is who we are, some more, some less, because of Bena. When the scientists are one day able to reconstruct from our DNA, or from whatever, the whole of our experience, are able to discern through a microscope every detail of our biographies, they'll find traces of Bena in all of us, not just where memory is stored but in the very structures that define who we are. Maybe that's the way it always is, each human being changed by all the people with whom his life, her life, intersects. For sure that is the way it was and is for those of us whose lives met Bena's, doubly so for those whose lives were richly intertwined with hers. . . .

Comes the hardest question: How do you make sense of what's befallen us, this senseless story that has no moral? And the answer is, of course, you don't, you can't, you mustn't even try. That's not the way the world works; sometimes the system simply crashes. There are no "if only"s here, there's no relationship whatever between merit and reward; logic betrayed, faith betrayed, justice betrayed, Bena betrayed.

And yet: I've thought about that a lot this week, and while there's plainly no lesson in the ending we have witnessed, this week that so abruptly and inexplicably and unreasonably ends a life so filled with energy, so engaged, so thorough, is not without its comfort, inadequate as such comfort in such circumstance must be and remain. Here I speak for myself alone, yet I'd be surprised if others do not share the thought. There's high drama in the roller coaster vigil, there's an extraordinary intensity, the mix of terrifying anticipation and urgent hope, but throughout the careening ride, from last Sunday morning when we learned that it was crisis time through the downs and the downs and the fleeting ups, through a Thursday that broke our hearts, through that endless day when the dying ripened into death and, endless, ended . . . we, all of us, loving Bena all, came to love each other in new ways. For the family, I know it is so. New respect, new affection, new thoughtfulness one for the other, a new appreciation of each other's strengths, and of our weaknesses as well, a heightened awareness of each other's value.

Now it comes time to begin the awful task of transforming the vital presence into a vivid memory. We take Bena to her grave, hard by where two of her grandparents lie, Rashi's parents and mine, who in the muteness of death will never understand why it's Bena who's come to them first; we pause for some days, and then slowly we take up the threads, return to work and to responsibility, return, however hurt, to life. Perhaps now that we have so closely witnessed the harsh ephemerality of life we may return to a life lived not just with the honesty and the energy that we learn from Bena's life but also with an extra measure of respect, of affection, of gentle thoughtfulness one for another, family and friends alike. So if now we must return to a world made smaller by her absence from it, perhaps it can also be made, perhaps we can also make it, a world enlarged and enriched by what we've learned and what we've felt during this week of awful sorrow.

That's not the bargain we would have chosen, but it's what we have, and it's not nothing.

And now it is time for the unveiling of Bena's stone. For Rachel and Jessica and Zelda, it will be their first visit to the cemetery since Nomi's funeral. I have counseled David not to come, and he has so chosen. Weeks before the appointed day, the awareness of its imminence settles on us all. And so, the Sunday before, I drive to the cemetery myself. Perhaps this will somehow make me stronger next Sunday, when the family will gather.

My friend Ken, whose son died at seventeen after a year-long illness, every week visits the cemetery where his son is buried. I prefer this writing, or other ways of remembering. Perhaps, too, I prefer a kind of forgetting. I do not fear that I will ever forget that which I want very much to remember: Nomi, alive. Here in the cemetery, though it is a particularly beautiful place, the fact of her death is unbearable, for here, beneath this scar in the grass, the grass that has not yet fully grown over the dirt that just eighteen weeks ago I and those I love and those she loved shoveled to cover my daughter's casket, here she is. (Again, the mincing euphemism. I must say the word: coffin.) How can I not talk to her, to a Nomi who cannot hear me? How can I stop myself from visualizing her? How can I not want to tear out the earth with my hands and reach her, buried?

That is what I feel when I come alone. The next Sunday there are some thirty of us, come to be with Bena. Almost all of us, it seems, have chosen to arrive well in advance of the appointed hour. We mill about in greeting and in casual conversation, some distance from the graves where Bena, Nomi, and my parents lie. Hesitantly, now one, now two of us break away and approach the graves. Finally, we make a circle around them. My brother says a few words. His words touch me, but now, just a few days later, I cannot recall them, not at all, save that he acknowledges the miserable fact that both these young women lie here, so very close to one another, and are so untimely gone. And it occurs to me that even together, they did not have the years we are entitled to expect. Bena was thirty-four, Nomi, thirty; together, not even the three score and ten we are promised. Another broken promise.

Karen sings a song she has written to/for Bena, the ritual prayers are recited, and we all return to my home to accomplish the transition back to "normal" life. People eat, and chat, and, in time, laugh, and the event passes without anyone having broken down, without the acuteness we had anticipated.

The honey and the thorn

When everyone has left, now mid-afternoon, and I am alone, I am desolate. Yesterday, I received from a friend of Nomi's a collection of letters Nomi had sent to her from Israel. Jessie does not want me to read them. "An invasion of Nomi's privacy," she says. I cannot quarrel with her, but I am drawn to reading them. I want to know what I can about my daughter.

No, it is more precisely that there will be no new data as time goes by, no future. So I am reduced to delving into the past. That, I suppose, is why I am so charmed by the stories her friends tell me. And that is why I will read her letters. And whether it is my chronically flawed memory or that Nomi did not share these things with me, I learn much from them. I learn, among other things, that the reason she decided to leave anthropology is that "it started to seem like a pretty isolated, esoteric field without any real direct influence on people. With the kind of anthro that I'm interested in—conflict resolution—the idea of studying a group's problems just to explain them to college kids who probably don't care all that much, seems like an intermediary role. So, I think, I may get a second Master's, either in education or public policy, which I think may be more useful in a direct 'hands-on' way."

Odd. We must have discussed that, it's very much the sort of thing we would have discussed. No matter. Much else in the letters is familiar. Nomi and some friends had gone off to Kenya, and when she returned, David—with whom she was living—had rented a piano as a surprise. The letters tell about that, and about her brief flirtation with the idea of dropping her academic studies for a while and studying piano full-time. And they tell, most sweetly, of her ripening love for David, and about her trip to Budapest with me. I'd been invited to lecture there, and the invitation came with a ticket for a "significant other," and my hosts were pleasantly agreeable when I asked that they assign that ticket to my daughter. We met, feeling very much the jet-setters, in the Zurich airport, flew on to Budapest together, and there, almost from the start, she fell in with a group of Hungarian college students who—it was 1990—were experiencing the excitement of the beginning of Communism's fall. (Not atypically, one of them developed a solid crush on Nomi, and wrote to her for some months thereafter. Such crushes were entirely par for her course.) Before parting some days later at the Zurich airport, we drove through the Alps for two days.

On the one hand, these letters, so lively, so filled with anticipation, Nomi in all her manifold parts and enthusiasms. On the other hand, that very morning, her grave.

It is not possible to relish the memories without experiencing the sorrow; the honey and the thorn. That is now and forever a given. I have a copy of the wedding video, and this coming Sunday is Nomi and David's anniversary. I want to watch the video, but I am afraid to, and I wonder if and when I will feel myself able to watch it. Some say that time will heal; I know only that time will change the ways in which I experience Nomi's absence. But knowing this offers no special comfort, since time cannot be rushed, since I do not know in what ways the experience will be changed, above all since the fact of the matter will not change. Not ever.

God?

I am not an expert on death. Perhaps there are such experts. Perhaps those who work with terminally ill patients, or battlefield medics—perhaps they have a closer understanding of what it means to die, or if not of what it *means* then at least of what it is *like*. But even they, it seems to me, can only know about the act of dying, not about the state of being dead. Yes, there is a literature on near-death experiences, people who claim that they have entered the kingdom of death but somehow turned back. Rejected by death, as it were, before they got all the way in. So even if we credit their experience, it is not especially informative. The blazing light and sweet music they report may just as well be the mark of the end as the sign of a new beginning. Of death itself we continue to know exactly nothing, save that it is not life.

Death is incomprehensible. When a parent dies "in the fullness of time," we may not consider the unfathomable mystery of death very closely. We understand, however much we may avoid thinking about it, that our lives are brief passages, and the death of a parent is in accord with "the nature of things." But when a child dies, the shock, the radical disorientation the death provokes, force the consideration upon us. What does it mean to be dead?

I think the reason we cannot fight our way through the tangles of our thoughts is that death is forever, and we cannot comprehend what "forever" means. "Forever" is infinite, and the one thing that human beings are barred from truly understanding is infinity. Take the very largest number you can imagine, and then add another; if you can (but how can you?), then add another, and then another, and, when you're all done, really and finally done, know that infinity is beyond even that. Infinity is not the end; it is the end plus one. (One definition of God: God is the only being that comprehends infinity.) Nothing that we know prepares us to handle "forever." Yet that is precisely what death is about.

Perhaps the clash between what we can understand and the experience of death is what accounts for doctrines of resurrection or of reincarnation. We rebel, quite understandably, against the genuinely incomprehensible forever, and so we deny it.

Before all this, I might here have written, "But I have no such illusions." Now, I cut more slack for those who cling to them. While they mean nothing to me, my concern is less for intellectual responsibility than it is for solace. If people imagine a soul that survives, or even a body that will one day rise up from death, and take comfort from such imaginings, so be it. I will not quarrel with them or even think less of them for their repair to what I regard as magical thinking.

God? No God of which (of whom?) I can conceive wills the death of an innocent. (Every time a survivor of a plane crash or other calamity in which others have died says, "God was looking out for me" or some such, I cringe. If God was looking out for them, does that mean that God had it in for the others, those who didn't survive?) No, God is not an interventionist.

The bleakest example in our own time is, of course, the Holocaust, that unbearable challenge to naïve faith and, it occurs to me, to sophisticated faith as well. How can a God that is both all-good and all-powerful have failed to intervene during those years? It is one thing to say that even God cannot attend to all the details of what happens here, cannot so monitor highway traffic as to keep apart two cars headed for a collision. It is quite another to say that God was too busy to notice the death of six million Jews during the time of the Kingdom of Night. But in theory, numbers don't matter to God; a compassionate God to whom we pray cares for us one by one. The death of one child, the ravaging sickness of one adult, the indignities of one aged person—all of these, each of these, is, in theory, of concern to God. Yet surely we have by now sufficient evidence that, whether concerned by one person's suffering or only by the suffering of many, God does not translate that concern into action.

Nomi and I talked about God from time to time. She was overtly more observant than I, but believed, as do so many people when pressed for definition, in God as "the force for good in the world," or as a First Cause, or as some other decidedly nontraditional and assuredly nonliteral being. By and large, we agreed that one experiences God through one's relations with human beings, that the closest we can come to God is through *imitatio dei,* the imitation of God's attributes—which is to say, through ethical behavior. "To know God," says Emmanuel Levinas, the French Jewish philosopher, "is to know what must be done." In that sense, feeding the hungry is a form of worship. (In Hebrew, the word *"avodah"* means "service," both in the sense of "work" and in the sense of "worship.") Yet there is a kinship between the two. And when, for whatever the reason, we cannot or do not start from God, there is another starting point—our knowledge of "what must be done." Does that not amount to the same thing, for all practical (and other) purposes?

And yes, I am aware of the danger of arguing from "what must be done." There's little doubt, for example, that those who have committed terrible acts of violence in opposing abortion believe, sincerely and with certainty, that they are doing God's will, doing what must be done. Worse yet, they perceive themselves as acting ethically. How can I assert that what I "know" is more faithful or more ethical or more godly than what they claim to know? What "proof" can either of us bring? Our assessments are inherently subjective, and all we have to work with are arguments, not evidence. So as seductive as the Levinas formulation at first blush seems, it is grossly inadequate. It is only about process, not about substance. Regarding process, it teaches that God is about a way of being and behaving rather than (merely) a way of believing. The nature and substance of the being and the behaving we must derive from other sources.

All that is quite different from the classic consolation, often illustrated by the story of Beruriah, the wife of Rabbi Meir. Their two sons died while Rabbi Meir was in the synagogue. When he came home, and only after he recited the prayers that mark the end of the Sabbath and she gave him his evening meal, Beruriah said to him, "I have a question to ask you. Not long ago, some precious jewels were entrusted to my care. Now the owner has come to reclaim them. Shall I return them?"

"Of course," her husband replied. It was only then that she took Rabbi Meir to her room and removed the sheet with which she had covered the two boys. Rabbi Meir burst into tears, calling out, "My sons! My sons!" And Beruriah, herself in tears, reminded him: "Did you not say that we must restore to the Owner that which He entrusted to our care? Our sons were the jewels that God left with us, and now their Master has taken back his very own."

I think that story close to blasphemy, for it depicts a capricious God. Capricious. Why else suddenly call in a loan that, according to convention, was to last at least three score years and ten? Was I an unworthy borrower? Was Nomi fatally deficient? No. Though it is certain that I have been imperfect in my efforts to live an honorable life, and it is possible (though doubtful) that Nomi, too, fell short, there is Liat, still innocent. I do not claim that I "owned" Nomi, but that is not because I believe she was merely lent to me, to us. It is because no parent owns his or her child. Nomi was a person unto herself; she was not ours, neither as loan nor as possession. Before she was taken from me and from her mother, she was taken from herself. (I will be reminded of that again and again, at least for now, as I find myself miserable in the face of great beauty—say, for example, during the last act of *La Traviata*—and realize the specific cause of my sorrow is that Nomi will never see or hear that which moves me so and which doubtless would have caused her comparable pleasure.) When, these days, I spend time with Liat, her sweetness begets bitterness on Nomi's behalf: How much pleasure Nomi would have derived from her daughter. Where is the parable that can dissolve the bitterness, that can gentle it away?

So let us leave God out of this, lest we be provoked not to pious acceptance but to heretical anger.

Unless . . . unless I repair here, with reference to God, to the words I used earlier to describe life without Nomi: "The enduring presence of an absence."

Theodicy: good people, bad things

I am scarcely the first to be brought to a halt by the vexing question of God's goodness, of how if at all we can reconcile our idea of God with a universe so riddled with evil, with sorrow. Whole libraries have been devoted, and continue to be, to the theodicy question, the question that asks how we can understand evil if God is good, injustice if God is just—or how we can understand God in a world of much injustice and much evil. For some, the answer is deism, belief in a God who created the world and then abandoned it. Others posit an absolutely consistent God, who once having promised freedom, cannot intervene, no matter the provocation. Once, many people imagined a God in competition with a Satan, a God therefore responsible only for the good things. None of these seems adequate to me. But what is the alternative? A God who by rational calculus decides that a child should die?

Accordingly, the God of whom I speak, whose name I do from time to time invoke, is the central character in an elaborate metaphoric system. Such a God neither makes things right nor explains any of life's mysteries. Such a God, far from providing answers to questions that otherwise cannot be answered, comes to ask questions that might otherwise be forgotten, questions such as: Where are you? Where is your brother? Or: How can you sing when My children are drowning?[1]

Then what of prayer? Not the prayer for intercession; in Nomi's case, there was no time for such prayer. (Had there been, I have no doubt all of us would have had recourse to it,

---

[1] The reference is to the *midrash* that tells of God's response to the angels, who burst into triumphant song when the waters covered over the Egyptian horsemen who were pursuing the fleeing Israelite slaves.

some because they believe in its utility, more because of the "foxhole religion" phenomenon—"it couldn't hurt," as they say—and at least one, I myself, because that is the form of expression that comes most naturally and most poignantly in moments of great crisis.) Here, the issue is the prayers that our ritual prescribes in the aftermath of a death—the prayers of the daily service, which are recited in the home for a week and in the synagogue for the next three weeks, and the specific prayers of the mourner. What, for example, of the prayer—part of the daily ritual—in which we praise God "who brings life to the dead"?

At first, those words grated, and I was unable to speak them, even as metaphor. Later, as I came to understand the diverse ways in which memories of Nomi live on, in which her story continues to unfold, I accepted their truth. But the truth value of the words is not, more generally, my principal concern. The function of prayer (as I understand it) is not intellectual but affective. Does it ease pain and nurture hope to stand as a member of a historic community in a ritual recitation? One is not required to perceive the world through a jeweler's glass, rigorously scrutinizing each event and each word for its compatibility with logic. Descartes was very wrong with his "I think, therefore I am"; what distinguishes the human being, what constitutes our "is-ness" and dignifies us beyond the Cartesian model, is precisely the connection between thinking and feeling. No apology whatever is required for affect, nor need we feel that we are, somehow, "indulging" our weakness when we repair to it.

That is why I recite the kaddish, our prayer for the dead. The kaddish is an ancient prayer that Jews have recited for many centuries, and so it reminds and reassures me that I am not alone in the experience of tragedy, of loss. I recite it because other mourners rise to join me in its recitation, or, as in some synagogues, the entire congregation rises in commiseration as it is recited. I recite it because the rhythm of its words is so evocative, even as the words themselves hold no meaning for me, at least until I come to the end, where we ask of God "who has made peace up above" to make peace here, for us. And when, after the year of mourning is concluded, I am no longer counted among the ritual mourners, I miss the embrace of the routine.

And that is also why, at the bottom of Nomi's gravestone, the Hebrew initials that are traditional are etched, the initials that stand for the words, "May her soul be bound up in the bond of life." May that be God's will.

While it is true that we must give one another space, each to grieve in his or her own way, the formulaic rituals of mourning are an exquisite comfort. Most obviously, they relieve the mourner of the responsibility for a dozen and more decisions in the immediate aftermath of the loss, at a time when shock and grief render decision-making especially difficult. It almost doesn't matter what specific rituals are prescribed, so long as the mourner is part of a tradition or culture that provides norms for the time of mourning.

Beyond the relief from responsibility, ritual has a different and more subtle function. You do not have to compose a prayer; the prayer is there for you, as it has been for generations. The fact that there are rituals means that what you are experiencing is not new, is not unprecedented. While your loss is unique, it is also not unique; countless others have experienced what you now experience. That insight, implicit in the ritual, brings comfort not because misery loves company, but because many, perhaps most, of those countless others have gone on with their lives. Although you know your life will never be the same, neither is it over.

Memory

In fact, it is not a betrayal of the one who died or evidence of hard-heartedness that the heavy quilt of mourning reduces in time to a throw across one's life. Tearless hours, days, then even weeks, do not bespeak a shallowness of sorrow. There is work to be done, much work, and there are others to nurture, to embrace, to discover, still others to block and to blunt. Nor is it all sober responsibility. There is wonder, and there's laughter, art and kindness not only to encourage but to behold. We do not break our lines to weep, wrote Yeats. Nor can we halt the play itself, even if we are allowed a weeklong absence from the stage. Nor should we, lest death's bounty be magnified. Death, as life, comes to us (mostly) from outside ourselves, an unearned gift bestowed, a sentence, deserved or not, decreed. All we have is what's between the two—our freedom, our hopes. Our tiny present tense. Life. And the lines we choose to speak—now, in the wake of loss, to speak defiantly.

That said, there's a feeling of guilt when the quilt becomes a throw, when a day or even two go by without active remembering. Is this not the sign of a double dying? If we do not attend the letters, how will they be brought to blossom? If we laugh, do we not abandon? How serious can we be if we dare to rise from our mourning and "go on"? But death, it turns out, is the only constant in this ongoing transaction. The grief is one day a wisp, one day a whirlwind. The memory is one day piercing, another day gentle. I am one day bereft, another day my bereavement is reduced from whole to part. In any case, it is a mistake to imagine that Nomi "lives" only if and as she is actively and explicitly remembered, that we dishonor her when we fail to activate our memory of her. And here there are no pretty words with which to conclude the thought: Whether actively remembered or neglected, it's all the same. She does not live. And we, who do, must do the best we can to come to terms with her absence.

Context

This morning's paper reports on a twenty-six-year-old woman in New York who is lying in a coma from which she may not recover after having been attacked, in broad daylight, in Central Park. As last year's paper did, as next year's paper will. I cannot imagine what torture this poor young woman's parents, who were on vacation somewhere out west, are experiencing. As so many parents and siblings and mates have experienced, and will. And not, obviously, only on account of crime, but also of war and of pestilence and of famine, of flood and of accident and of terrorist madness. My daughter died quietly. At most, the doctor tells me many months later, when I have finally felt ready to talk with him about her death, she experienced a momentary dizziness before losing consciousness: a death without a dying. What an enduring assault it must be for parents who know that their child's last moments were spent in pain or in terror, with full awareness that they were about to die.

I wonder whether here in America—all things considered, so stable a nation-state—we are led to have a misplaced confidence in our prospects and in the prospects of our loved ones. What is it like for a parent in Rwanda, where death is a daily terror? What was it like in Cambodia, or in Somalia, or in Srebrenica, in far too many places? When death, less exceptional, happens there, is the heart less broken? I do not think so. And then: So what? In the end there is no point to this consideration of comparative hurt and grief; whatever the cultural and personal particulars, we are a vast company, we mothers and fathers who have buried a child.

When the buses in Israel were bombed a month after Nomi died, I experienced something that felt strangely close to envy. At the time, I thought I was childishly wishing that the death we'd all experienced had had some drama to it. But now I understand it better: What I wanted was for the death, if death there had to be, to be part of a larger story. And perhaps that is also why from nearly the very first moment on learning the terrible news, even though the death was not in fact part of any larger story, I felt so strongly the need to "explain" to the hospital chaplain—and to myself—that, as I wrote much earlier, I felt no shock. "Gaping loss, but not shock," I wrote. "Death itself, even untimely death, the death of a child—these are not, after all, strangers, not to anyone in our century, surely not to a Jew who has internalized the history of his people." That was my way of seeking context, of finding a story into which to insert what had happened. And even now, these many months later, I do not regard that search as far-fetched. It was not mortality I was trying to defeat; that would have been pointless. It was, rather, randomness. (Yes, of course it's true that death by terrorist bomb—this bus rather than the next bus—is random. But the terrorism itself fits, alas, into a larger context. So, too, death by AIDS, or at the hands of a drunken driver.)

I understand the urge for context, for a hospitable story—and I understand the dangers of that urge. A larger story can be a way of depersonalizing that which remains the only thing we really own, our own biographies. Hannah Arendt tell us that "The history of any given personality is far older than the individual as product of nature, begins long before the individual's life, and can foster or destroy the elements of nature in his heritage." But to search for cosmic significance by placing oneself inside a larger story is to risk losing oneself inside that story, thereby coming face-to-face with our own insignificance.

There's another issue here as well, one that I feel especially keenly. I write, I lecture, and that means that everything is grist for my literary mill. Do I thereby stand outside the events of my own life? Am I hereby converting this most terrible event into "just" another story, an especially compelling story that serves the twin purpose of neutralizing it and, heaven forbid, of dazzling the audience, the reader? Is this in some awful sense the story of "my own private Auschwitz"? The story of Nomi not as a story worthy in its own right, nor as a memorial nor a gift to Liat, not even as a cathartic exercise, but because it adds poignant drama to my own story? I shudder to think that a possibility, yet I cannot be certain.

Or perhaps it is all of the above. The stories we live are plural. People are frightfully complicated, and even the people we think we know well, those whose stories seem entirely coherent, straightforward narratives, live other stories, too. This is most obvious in the case of politicians, who generally put forward a "main" story that is manufactured, contrived, one that may have very little to do with the genuine story of their lives—that is, until the contrivance becomes so instinctive that they themselves cease to discern the boundary between their several stories. In some measure, the same is true of all public people. I used to think that one of my gifts as a public speaker is my openness with my audiences, the unusual degree to which I share myself with them. And then one day it came to me that between me and them there is a podium, a podium that enables me to control quite precisely the nature and degree of the sharing. The stories I've told have always been true; most people's stories are. But they've also been only the stories I've chosen to share, selected from among the several and sometimes (often?) competing truths of my life. The other stories and their truths I've shared very, very selectively, if at all. And it's been work not to perceive myself as, in some measure, I've chosen to cause other people to perceive me.

In any case, all this talk of stories has a built-in limitation. A thousand threads converge, meet in one person's life, and then, rewoven by that person, continue on, meet in different combinations in another person's life. There is, indeed, an aspect of immortality to that; in that sense, too, there is death without dying. But in the end, the corporeal person, the entirely unique person who is defined as much by the particular convergence of stories that has never happened before and never will again as much as by the DNA that is hers and hers alone—that combination of mind and body comes to an end with death. And even if we were able to catalogue all of each person's stories, we would no more have recreated that person than if we were to draw (as soon we will be able to) a complete map of that person's DNA.

So I am under no illusion here. These stories do not add up to Nomi. They are, simply, what is left to me. And Nomi's story, for all the heartbreak in which it is embedded, stands utterly alone, is not part of any larger story, has no cushioning context. One day, absurdly, she died.

A hypothetical
And if she had not lived?

Now and again I am drawn to ask: What if the flaw in her heart had been discernable while her mother was carrying her? What, that is, if the doctors had come to us then—say, in the third month of her mother's pregnancy—and said, "Your unborn daughter has a heart condition. While she will be able to live a normal life, there is a high probability that at some point, perhaps when she's 10, or 20, or 30, she will suddenly die." Would we have opted for an abortion?

In the abstract, if I'd been given this problem without a name attached to it—say, for example, if someone had put the question to me as an intellectual exercise a year or more ago—I'd surely have endorsed an end to the pregnancy. Why bring into this world a new person who must from birth live sentenced to an untimely death? Abort, and try again.

But Nomi was hardly an abstraction. Had that been our choice, we'd never have known her. How, in retrospect, deny life to her, how abort her story, how diminish the stories of others to which she added, thereby expunge Liat's story, too? Better an interrupted life than no life; better a Nomi gone so long before her time than no Nomi.

But wait: If we'd known up front what lay in store, then we'd likely have been different parents, always wondering which day might be her last. And at some point, we'd have been obliged to share the information with her. What kind of life would that have been for her? Would she have dared marry, have children?

I am relieved that such questions are hypothetical, concerned that our developing technologies may soon make them real, even urgent, for people no better equipped than I to struggle through them.

Jessie

Jessie works nearby, and we often have lunch together. Her first book is out in just a few months, she's working on the proposal for its sequel, she's developing an idea for a new magazine. These are the things, by and large, we talk about.

But from time to time one of us will ask a version of the "How are you doing?" question. One day, I try to explain to her that my developing love for Liat is no substitute for my love for Nomi, that I do not see Nomi in Liat, that I want to be close to Liat more for her sake than for my own—as a link to the mother she can only know at second hand, and to earlier generations she could in any case not have known, and perhaps also because I have some things I think worth teaching, passing on. And Jessie says, "The reason I want to be really, really close to Liat is so that she can absorb whatever Nominess there is in me."

I love her for thinking that, for saying it. And while I am utterly incapable of judging Jessie's "Nominess," I am glad, too, for Liat's sake, glad beyond measure that she will at least be granted a healthy dose of Jessiness. And at the end of a day during which I called her at work to share with her a condolence letter I'd just received, she says, ever so gently, "Dad, unless you really need to, it would be better if you didn't call me at work with things like that. Unless you really need to." And I love her for that, too. And I know that in some ways, Nomi's death is hardest of all on her, for she is the only one save for Liat who has never until now, not for a single day, known a world without Nomi in it. And also because there is likely no relationship in the world quite as intimately textured as the relationship between two sisters who are also best friends.

And there is so very little I can do to ease her way.

A year goes by

Fifty weeks later, and we approach the first anniversary of Nomi's death, the *yahrzeit*. The preceding many months have been especially crowded. I have taken on new work that keeps me away from Boston much of the time, Jessie and Rob became engaged, and Liat turned two. For her birthday party, we gathered at Rachel's, the apartment suitably decked out with streamers and balloons; all of us, and I especially, went wildly overboard in the presents we bought her. Liat had a wonderful time, and the party was as sad an event as I can recall, each new cuteness and precocity a new clamp on the heart. Where was Nomi, who birthed this darling little girl, Nomi who more than any had earned the right to feel gladness and without whom the gladness was so constricted?

In July, I'd traveled to Israel and met there with Nomi's friends from her time in Jerusalem, and in August we had the unveiling of the stone, and in October I listened to Brahm's German Requiem, to the words "Death, where is thy sting?" and knew quite precisely where it is, and finally in December I got beyond the need to tell even cabdrivers and salesclerks about Nomi. Or is it about myself that I have been telling them, their customer the bereaved? Why? And the question answers itself: For months, being the father of a dead daughter has been the most organizing aspect of my identity. Now that has begun to change.

And, increasingly, as the months go by, dreams of Nomi, good dreams in the main, until I awake and she is gone again, still.

A dream: I am in the vestibule of an apartment building. It is dark outside, and raining. I see her, standing in the rain, wearing a parka. She approaches the house, enters the vestibule. We hug, fiercely. And then she tells me, "Dad, I am going to die." We cry, and I awaken.

An anniversary surprise

And then, inexorably, the first *yahrtzeit*. The night before, I red-eye back from California. I have told Rachel and Jessie that I will be going to the cemetery, and that they are, of course, welcome to come with me. They have checked with their mother; she, too, wants to come. I cannot quarrel with her decision, even though I'd hoped she'd decline. We have been divorced for twenty-three years and have long since become strangers to each other. More precisely: We talk as need or occasion warrants, but until now there's too often (though not always) been an edge to our interaction; I fear the visit to the cemetery will be brief and awkward.

But that is not how it turns out, not at all. We meet at the cemetery, stand around the grave, and quite suddenly find ourselves talking about Jessie's upcoming wedding, and then Zelda and I engage in friendly reminiscence, not so much of the years with Nomi as of the years before. We laugh with the remembering, and forty minutes soon pass. Not strangers, after all. In retrospect, though there was no consciousness of it at the time, we were bringing Nomi up to date.

They say that the death of a child often puts an unbearable strain on the marriage of that child's parents. Guilt and blame, different modes of coping, different trajectories for healing, two mourners cast together, each with little energy to console the other. I know couples who, unable to handle the strain, have separated in the wake of their child's death, and others whose marriages have become a frozen torture. Here, however, the marriage is a distant memory. There is nothing between us that requires preservation, and it is to others we turn for consolation. Yet death trumps the neat legality of a divorce decree; we remain connected, and the connection has suddenly been rendered immediate. What we now share we share with no other, for it is not that we have, both of us, lost a child; we have, both of us and no one else, lost *this* child. The result seems to be that we approach one another with deference, with empathy. And now at graveside, even with a touch of intimacy.

And later, both Rachel and Jessie will observe that this is the first time in many, many years—perhaps ever since the divorce, twenty-three years back—that they and their parents have been together with no others present.

Inside the sadness

Some people had said, back during the active condolence phase, that in due course the good memories would displace the bad. No—or, at any rate, not yet. There are no bad memories, except of the day death entered our lives, creating the absence that remains, and will. The good memories coexist with that absence, and sharpen it. You cannot fill a void by sweeping all the good stuff into it; a void is bottomless, and whatever you try to fill it with is lost, leaving only the empty space you started with. The most and the best that you can try to do is avoid spending all your time staring into that empty space, so that life, in all its complex richness of memory and commitment, can proceed.

What has changed in these months is this: For a time, I lived inside the sadness; now I live with it.

Closure?

There is much talk, these days, of "closure." Relatives of a murder victim, we are told, cannot achieve closure until the murderer is caught, tried, and punished.

How odd. "Closure," it seems to me, is something you achieve when, after an argument that got out of bounds, you talk the matter through more calmly with the person you've argued with and put the argument behind you. You can put closure to your resentments. But how can you put closure to your losses, save by making them good? And how do you make good a loss-by-death?

True, I do not confront a situation that occasions resentment. There is no one to blame. But if there were someone to blame? If, for example, the cardiologist had erred, had failed to diagnose and treat a condition that should have been diagnosed and treated, would his conviction on grounds of malpractice, or even his death, have offered me closure? Hardly. It would, I suppose, have offered me sullen satisfaction. But closure? Not only is closure not possible; it is not appropriate. What can it possibly mean? That things have now been set right, the score evened up? That now what happened did not happen, or that it no longer matters that it happened, or that the loss has been fully compensated for?

The essential nature of this kind of loss is that it endures, it can never be made good. I do not apologize for the tears, and would deem it unnatural were they to stop. I do not want or need a therapist to "treat" me for my grief; I grieve for good and sufficient reason. The texture of the grief may change in time, or not. Others may cut me less slack for my grief as the months and years pass; no matter. I will grieve as I am disposed to grieve, and I will not rush to place the grief in a cupboard, to be taken out from there only on ritual occasions.

A Passover reading

A second Passover has come and gone. At our Passover seder, we intersperse the readings with music from a tape that I've compiled over the years—mostly, traditional lyrics to an array of melodies reflecting the very different places our people have lived and have sung these words. The "honey and the thorn" song with its plea to God "not to uproot that which has been planted" is among our several nontraditional additions to the tape, and now we've quite carefully marked it so that we will not by mistake play even a tiny piece of it. But what shall we do with the reading that Nomi was the one to read at our seder table ever since she was eight or nine years old—and read, all those years, with pride and with conviction? It's the familiar section from Anne Frank's diary:

It's really a wonder that I haven't dropped all my ideals, because they seem so absurd and impossible to carry out. Yet I keep them, because in spite of everything I still believe that people are really good at heart. I simply can't build up my hopes on a foundation consisting of confusion, misery, and death. That's the difficulty in these times: ideals, dreams, and cherished hopes rise within us, only to meet the horrible truth and be shattered.

I see the world gradually being turned into a wilderness. I hear the ever-approaching thunder, which will destroy us, too. I can feel the suffering of millions—and yet, if I look up into the heavens, I think it will come out alright, that this cruelty too will end, and that peace and tranquility will return again.

In the meantime, I must uphold my ideals, for perhaps the time will come when I shall be able to carry them out.

No, not this year. Nor next. Yet I am confident that the words will eventually make their way back to our ceremony. They will be read out loud again when Liat is old enough to understand them. She deserves no less. And perhaps I will be blessed to live long enough to hear Liat herself read them at our Passover table. If so, there will no doubt be tears. But there will also be the warmth that comes of being present at a miracle, the miracle of a story—a life?—that continues.

A meditation

Given what happened to Anne Frank, given what has happened to so many people in so many places in the years since Anne's death, the temptation is to attribute her sentiment— "people are really good at heart"—to her innocence, and to note, with bitter sorrow, that had she known when she wrote those words how very soon her end would come, and with what indignity, she would surely have been cured of her naïveté.

I think of this as I wrestle with a death under totally different circumstances. All that connects Anne and Nomi is their foreshortened lives—and a paragraph one wrote, the other read. Still, it has become important to me to know that the words that Nomi read each year at our seder table were true, that she was not misled.

The arrest that followed the betrayal of the Frank family's Secret Annex came in early August of 1944, just nineteen days after Anne wrote of people's goodness. Four days later, she was transferred to Westerbork, the transit camp to which the Nazis sent virtually all Dutch Jews before moving them eastward, to the extermination camps of Poland.

And then, on September 3, 1944, as part of a group of 1,019 people, she was sent to Auschwitz on what would prove to be the last transport of Jews from Holland. Of that number, 549, including all the children under the age of fifteen, were gassed on September 6, the day they arrived. Anne and her sister, Margot, stayed in Auschwitz for less then two months before they were transferred to Bergen-Belsen. By now it was clear that the Germans had lost the war. Everywhere, the Russians were advancing, and conditions in all the camps were increasingly chaotic. In Bergen-Belsen, the combination of chaos and cruelty, along with bitter winter weather and the breakdown of the food supply, led to mass death—specifically, to a typhus epidemic that claimed tens of thousands of lives, Margot's and Anne's among them, Margot's a few days before Anne's, on or about March 31, 1945.

Now imagine that a Red Cross worker had come upon Anne as she lay dying and had asked her, frozen and feverish, hungry and humiliated, witness by now to the worst of man's designs, whether she still believed that "peace and tranquility will return again," whether she still believed, in spite of everything, "that people are really good at heart."

The question cannot be avoided. But the answer is not obvious. For perhaps by then Anne had also witnessed a behavior not at all uncommon during the terrible roll calls of Auschwitz, roll calls that required the prisoners to form up hours before dawn and stand at attention for two hours and more in their thin rags, through the rain and the snow, and then again in the evening, sometimes for three and four hours, now and then through the entire night. Some died on the spot, some contracted pneumonia, some fell from exhaustion. To fall and be noticed by an SS man meant to be beaten or shot. And so the practice among prisoners was to use their bodies to prop up those no longer able to stand.

Or perhaps Anne was witness to a story like the one that Gerda Klein tells, of how her friend Ilse came back from her job and "dug into her pockets. 'I have brought you a present!' she announced triumphantly. There, on a fresh leaf, was one red, slightly mashed raspberry." Or the prisoner who on her birthday received a green apple and "a used toothbrush from which the bristles had been worn off on one end."

Over and over again, detailed in countless memoirs and studies, we are brought up short: In the midst of the savagery, kindness; in the midst of the evil, good. If Anne knew of such behavior, how can we be certain she would have abandoned her view of human goodness? All that we can say for near certain is that her belief in human goodness, if indeed she retained it, would no longer have been the innocent view of a feisty fourteen-year-old. It would have been, instead, the stubborn view of one who has known the full scope of evil but who refused to substitute the part for the whole, who insisted instead on capturing the infinite complexity that is the human condition, good and evil, kindness and cruelty, the honey and the thorn.

The challenge goes well beyond an effort to search out an offsetting good for every evil, as if we might take the extreme examples of each and place them on the scales and hope and pray that the good might one day outweigh the evil. But the gray evidence of our daily lives reminds us that most of life cannot be so readily categorized, that people make terrible mistakes, even commit terrible evils, sometimes with the very best of intentions, that people can and often do "the right thing" for base motives, that some of us all of the time and all of us some of the time contain within ourselves seeds both bad and good. And that notwithstanding all the ambiguity and all the uncertainty and all the agony, we cannot, we dare not simply shrug our shoulders and let fate decide the outcome, we are bound to choose, we are bound to judge, and we are responsible for our judgments.

I have until now made no special reference to the fact that Anne was Jewish. No one can know what sort of a Jew she would have become had she survived. But I should like to think that whatever the particular formal shape of her identification, if indeed it would have had a formal shape, she would have discerned the heart of the Jewish understanding of these things. That understanding is far too complex to be derived wholly from our sacred texts; it is an understanding that begins with Genesis and is expanded and extended and transformed by the millennia of experience that are part of our collective memory.

Our texts and our history and our memory together teach two enduring lessons: First, that this world is not working the way it was meant to, that evil is far too often triumphant—and that to be a Jew is to understand that you are implicated in the world's repair, in what we call *tikkun olam*. And, second, that you cannot simply plant the seeds of good and leave them to grow on their own, that even though the very act of planting may take courage, may require of us a holy audacity, it is itself not sufficient. Once planted, the seeds must be tended and nurtured, and very often they must be irrigated with our tears.

In 1961, I attended some sessions of the trial of Adolph Eichmann in Jerusalem, and there came to understand that because in a system that rewards evil, many will choose to do evil, our task is to create systems that encourage and reward good: systems of politics and commerce, systems of culture and belief. We undertake the task even though we know how fragile such systems are, how truly painful are the choices we are called upon to make, how very often we will find good and evil hopelessly intertwined.

To create systems that encourage and reward good, and to hope. For in the end we are, we Jews, *assirei tikvah*, prisoners of hope. We suffer with all who suffer; we remember that we, too, were strangers once, and more than once; we remember the winding way through the desert; and we know there is not only a promised land but also a promised time. We know that they who plant in sorrow will surely one day reap in joy.

I have given much consideration to these things. I have, as have we all, daily confronted evidence of evil and daily have looked for countervailing evidence. And sometimes, that countervailing evidence does not have to be sought out, it is so near at hand. Sometimes, it is embodied in a simple exchange between two human beings.

I would like to think that God's own harsh judgment of the human condition—"man's devisings are evil from his youth"—would have been, perhaps in fact was, significantly modified upon reading the exchange of letters between Nomi and Sam Natansohn, that He was rendered repentant by the arguments they present and, more still, by the goodness they reflect. Nomi and Sam—exemplars of the good, prisoners of hope, refutations of God's harsh judgment. And perhaps, then, Anne Frank as well, witness to evil in its purest and most insistent form, witness as well, or so we may hope, to other Nomis and other Sams, would have explained that we live neither in the valley of the shadow of death nor atop the mountain of redemption, that we live instead in a desert of shifting sands where the best that we can do as we seek to cross to a better place and a better time is to press our bodies against those who falter and are about to faint, hold them close and upright until we come to the next resting place, there to regather our energy and then to resume our journey.

So yes: One day, Liat will read Anne's words, the true words her mother read, and the story will continue, the journey go on.

Terror

David has prepared a video, a composite of still photographs and selections from all the videos he'd shot from the time Nomi became pregnant with Liat until just days before she died. The video is intended for Liat. He had it put together professionally, and he's given each of us in the immediate family a copy.

My copy has been shelved, unwatched, for three months or more. At last, anxiously, I decide to watch it.

It is, of course, haunting, and I sob as I have not since Nomi died—huge, racking sobs. There is Nomi pregnant, and there is Liat moments after her birth. Several scenes—the baby-naming, a Hanukkah party—take place in my home. At the baby-naming, we all recite, "Blessed are You, Ruler of the universe, who has kept us alive, sustained us, and enabled us to reach this day." At the Hanukkah party, we light the candles and sing together. Happy times. And there, in another scene, Nomi, with Liat nearby, is playing the piano. This may be the only record we have of her playing, unless I can find, in a large box of unmarked tapes, the one I recorded during her recital when she was twelve.

The void, and the voice. That is what we have; that is what there is. Again and again, an isn't that is. Here I was about to add, "and an is that isn't," but that is not so. The "is" is not the corporeal Nomi. It is this video, and these memories, and these tears, and this Liat. And I am grateful for all of them.

But the terror is something else again. I have always been somewhat compulsive about the telephone, and the "some-what" is added here only for the sake of appearance. Still, I used to be able to let the phone ring on if, say, it started ringing as I had one foot out the door. Now I race back to grab it. Are Jessie and Rachel alright? A friend tries to persuade me that it's rude to interrupt a conversation to pick up on the "call waiting" signal. Sorry, there's no conversation I won't inter-rupt to hear who's calling, to make sure that everything is still as it is supposed to be, as once it was so bitterly not. The terror: I can no longer take my children's lives for granted.

Am I, then, paranoid? I think not. I do not expect the highly improbable to happen. But I can no longer rule out the possibility, the active possibility.

A wedding

We, all of us, were frightfully nervous before Jessie and Rob's wedding. It was only eighteen months after Nomi's death, and we weren't at all sure we could pull the wedding off with anything like the gaiety that weddings deserve. Nomi's absent presence, we feared, would weigh us down.

It was an outdoor wedding, and Liat, as the flower girl, followed the bridesmaids down the aisle. There was an intake of breath as she began, and sure enough, after just a few steps she stopped and looked around, confused. Just then, the music might as well have been the Funeral March. Rachel came quickly to the rescue, took Liat's hand and led her the rest of the way. But save for that brief moment, the rest of the procession was as it should have been, all of us determined to push against our apprehensions, to push open the doors to joy. And our guests, taking their cue from the family, feeling relief on our behalf and on their own, gave a bounce to the celebration that took us all to a place we hadn't been for many months, and feared we might never be again, a place where life vanquishes death. As it should.

David

In the Nomi and Liat video, there's an unseen participant. It is David, working the camcorder and instructing the stars; his voice can be heard off-camera. He has taken almost all the footage, and it is he, of course, who has arranged for its editing, as it is he who has assembled the letters to Liat into a lovely album. We are different, he and I: On the last page of that album, he has chosen to insert the *Ani Ma'amin,* the classic profession of absolute faith in the coming of the Messiah. I do not know whether he intends this literally or merely as a consoling metaphor; I know that the inclusion of so defiant a statement of faith would not have occurred to me.

David, as was Nomi, is more overtly and conservatively religious than I. More important, as I watch him in his new loneliness raise Liat, I am dazzled: He is a spectacular parent, offering his daughter a mix of love and discipline and challenge in magically appropriate combination. Instinct, medical training (he is a family physician), Nomi's example, whatever—Liat is most fortunate, as are we all. She grows delightfully.

And between her genetic endowment, her father's wisdom, Jessie's effort to transmit her own "Nominess," the hovering of the rest of us, she grows not only delightfully but Nomishly. This is confirmed by the report her day-care teachers prepare at the end of the 1998–99 school year: "She plays easily with friends, often offering ideas and solutions to problems. Recently one of the children was having a difficult time getting involved in the group. When we approached Liat, she welcomed him enthusiastically and the two played together for about half an hour." "The strength of Liat's cognitive engagement often results in her being a cornerstone in the group. She does not let other children's distraction get in her way and will often be the 'hook' to get the other children involved in a cognitively challenging activity." "Liat often helps friends set up or pack up their nap belongings."

I am more than pleased; I am charmed by these intimations of Nomi, these hints that of all the virtues a child might display, Liat's incipient virtues so closely mirror Nomi's. Genes? Perhaps. But there's a more proximate explanation. Last January, a few days before Nomi's third *yahrtzeit*, David called to invite me to spend the day of the *yahrtzeit* together with some of his friends and the rest of the family as volunteers at Rosie's Place, Boston's principal shelter for homeless women. And so it was, fifteen or twenty of us helping to prepare and serve lunch to some dozens of miserable women, an activity that rendered literal meaning to the phrase, "May her memory be for a blessing."

It is in these ways that a tradition is handed down and sustained. Nature, perhaps; nurture, surely. It is in these ways that Anne Frank's stubborn hope is vindicated. There was a reason that Nomi and David found and loved each other.

Interweavings

Threads that weave themselves into the story:

Soon after Nomi died, I took some words from a prayer and made them the title of a piece I wrote about her, and a man from Oklahoma whom I do not know read those words and responded to them with other words, and the words he taught me—"the parchment is consumed, and the letters blossom in the air"—are now engraved on my daughter Nomi's stone.

My dearest male friend is Euch (short for Eugene), whom I've known since he was sixteen and I was eighteen. He lived in Milwaukee, to which I traveled every Wednesday night from Chicago, where I was in college, there to lead a group of high school boys who belonged to Habonim, the Zionist youth movement in which I'd done much of my growing up. We'd talk about things that now seem strange—they didn't then—for a bunch of adolescent boys: say, for example, the relative merits of collective versus cooperative agricultural settlements in Israel. And then we'd watch Jack Webb in *Dragnet,* and finally we'd adjourn and end the evening at the Yankee Doodleburger. In 1953, we were all scheduled to leave for a year in Israel, I to the Institute for Youth Leaders From Abroad, Euch and several of the other Milwaukee boys to the Habonim Workshop.

A few months before our scheduled departure, Euch's parents were murdered in a holdup. He came with us to Israel nonetheless, but when our year was up, he chose not to return to America. Instead, he remained, and has lived all these years in Geva, one of Israel's oldest and most solidly established kibbutzim. There he met and married Ilana, who'd been born in Geva; there he and Ilana had three sons; there, after some years, he was accepted by the community in his own right and not merely as a newcomer who'd married a native; there he became in time the manager of Geva's principal industry, a factory for manufacturing valves, as well as manager of the Gevatron, perhaps Israel's most popular traditional folk choir; and there, in 1992, he received the news that Ilana had been killed in an auto accident.

We'd been buddies over the years, our ever-ripening friendship sustained by my relatively frequent trips to Israel and his to America in connection with his work. One January day in 1996, Euch and I were driving from Geva to Haifa when he popped a tape into the cassette player. "Listen to this," he said. "It's a crossover hit, and I think you'll like it." The song was a jazz rendition of one of Judaism's most awesome prayers, the *U'netaneh Tokef,* chanted during the High Holidays, a prayer that tells us that "on Rosh Hashanah it is inscribed and on Yom Kippur it is sealed, who shall live and who shall die, who at the appointed time and who before his time." I was taken with the setting, but thought no more of it until days later, back in Boston, on the evening of the day when we buried Nomi. (And yes, it still clamps my heart to write those last three words.)

Suddenly I remembered that months earlier an Israeli friend had sent me a tape with the words *"U'netaneh Tokef"* written on its case, along with a note urging me to listen to it. I hadn't, for one reason or another—but, recalling now that I had that tape, with words that had taken on a new and terrifying meaning, I listened to it and listened to it, again and again, through the whole week of mourning. That is the prayer whose closing words, *kachalom ya'uf,* "as a dream that vanishes," I then took as the title of the piece I wrote when Nomi died, the piece the good rabbi from Oklahoma read and that occasioned his "the parchment is consumed" letter to me.

In the spring of 1998, as Israel celebrated the fiftieth anniversary of its independence, Euch and his choir, the eighteen-member Gevatron, came on tour to America. They had a day off between gigs, and were not far from Boston. So we planned that they'd come to Boston for the day, I'd show them around, and then they'd be at my home for the evening. I invited a few friends and some members of the Zamir Chorale, Boston's own specialists in Jewish choral music.

I'd wondered whether I could persuade them to sing or whether they'd be so relieved to have a night off that they'd be happier just to sit around chatting. I needn't have wondered:

They came, electric keyboard and all, eager to sing, to sing without the constraints of a formal concert program. And, as a token of their appreciation for my hospitality, they gave me a copy of their latest CD. Glancing at its table of contents, I noticed that it included the *U'netaneh Tokef,* and I told one of the singers my *U'netaneh Tokef* story—the tape and its association with the week of Nomi's death, the article I wrote, the letter from Oklahoma, the words on Nomi's stone.

He turned to one of the others and said, "Hanoch, sing the *U'netaneh Tokef.*" And a tall, thin, white-haired member of the choir stood and delivered the by-now familiar rendition of the haunting prayer.

Later that evening, Euch filled me in on the background: The Gevatron includes people from two kibbutzim, Geva and—just down the road—Bet Hashitah. During the 1973 Yom Kippur War, eleven members of Bet Hashitah were killed in the fighting, a frightfully large number of casualties for a small kibbutz. Living on the kibbutz at the time was one of Israel's most popular "pop" composers, Ya'ir Rosenbloom. When Bet Hashitah decided to have Yom Kippur become its day of remembrance for the fallen eleven, Rosenbloom decided to reward the kibbutz's hospitality by creating a new rendition to the *U'netaneh Tokef* prayer. And he composed the music with his favorite tenor in mind, a Bet Hashitah member named Hanoch, who had earlier that same evening stood erect in my living room and sung the prayer.

Thus do the circles spread.

Just two months later, Jessie and Rob and I were in Israel, and on the Saturday night we spent at Geva, the members of the choir and their spouses gathered in the open-air café that Geva rents out for weddings and private parties, and there under an improbably starry Valley of Jezreel sky, we sang, songs from earlier and perhaps more naïve times, sang for three hours of a world that likely never was but now, nostalgia triumphant, felt so much sweeter and more innocent than our bloody and mendacious world, sang as if that sweet world were real and we its untroubled, unwounded citizens.

Thus do the threads weave themselves into a story. Thus do the circles overlap, grief and solace, hurt and healing fuse.

Four years later

It is the fourth anniversary of Nomi's death, but (and?) the reminders are everywhere, every day. Some are by now quite common, part of the texture of my life: I wince each time I see an ambulance marked as equipped with "advanced life support systems," I become enraged when cars don't make way for wailing ambulances. Across a busy street, I see her. I consider crossing the street. Of course I know it is someone else. But how can I be sure, really sure? Other reminders—most, in fact—come from unexpected sources, in unexpected forms. Just before I'm to be introduced to speak—a talk, a more formal lecture—someone will approach, introduce herself as a friend of Nomi's, tell me how close they were, how much she misses her. Now and then, people brightly ask after her, and I must tell them what happened, then comfort them. Once, when I introduced myself to a folksinger after a concert, she embraced me and said, "I loved Nomi so much." Somehow, I hadn't known, or had forgotten, that she and Nomi knew each other.

And just last night, Michelle called. Michelle was among Nomi's closest friends. I saw her several months ago in San

Francisco, and she told me then how very often she visits Nomi in her dreams, and how real those dreams are to her. And while I don't "believe" in such things, I wanted to hear every detail. Michelle gave birth last week, and this coming Saturday, which is the very date of Nomi's death, there will be a baby-naming ceremony for her new daughter, who will be called Naomi.

The most poignant and the most potent and the most present reminder is, of course, Liat. Liat begins her life with a wounded heart, deprived of the most natural resource of all, a mother's active love. There is no way around that. But there are ways through it. She is neither the first nor the last, and, as if nature seeks to compensate for its punishing negligence, some of this orphaned band seem particularly adept at love; they have gone on to love—and be loved—with an intensity and a grace that dazzle the rest of us. Love, after all, is not a liquid that is first poured into us, then, in equal measure, poured out. One drop—not always, but now and then—is sufficient to beget a cascade.

And Liat begins with much more than one drop. She has her father, and the rest of us; she has all those friends whose promise to look out for her, to embrace her in the name of her mother whom they loved, is binding. And she has, mediated through others as it tragically must be, the certain knowledge that she was loved without reservation by her mother, loved actively, enthusiastically—or, as Nomi would surely have described it, "amazingly."

Some of that she will be told; some she will have learned from the book of letters and remembrances that those who knew her mother sent on to us after her death and that David has so carefully arrayed for her, and from the video he compiled, in which Liat costars with Nomi and in which Nomi's delight in her shines through. And some of it she will, I expect, discern from reading what I have written here about her mother.

Still, there is no getting around the deprivation. There are so many things Nomi would have taught Liat, whether by example or more directly. Some of those things Liat will for always be and do without, for no one can replicate the specific person and the specific wisdom that was Nomi's gift and that would in turn have been her gift to Liat. Others of those things Liat will learn elsewhere, from other examples, from books, from her own experience, from those who love her. And, perhaps, from the pages that now follow, where I shall try to write down some of what should by all rights have been handed down according to the natural order, from one generation to the next, from mother to daughter, but which now, again and instead, fall to me to pass on to my progeny.

PART III

A Letter to Liat

LIAT, DEAR, SWEET LIAT:
You're five as I write; you'll likely be thirteen or so by the time you read this. By that time, God willing, you and I will have spent much time together, have had much chance to talk. So these words are not intended as a summary of all the things I hope one day to tell you, nor as a catalogue of answers to all the questions you will doubtless ask. They are just the words that are on my mind today, a day on which I approach the end of these pages about your mother, about me, and, therefore, about you.

For all the love that's been showered on you by family and by friends, your world has begun in disarray, a highly specific form of disarray. In the end, there is no way to compensate for so particular a loss, for the pain and the grief that are not about people-in-general but a specific person, one with a name, one with a smile that could be no other's. They say one should strive for perspective. Perspective? The details of this specific person—her smile, her gait, in your mother's case, her magic—crowd out perspective. In the cemetery, the other stones and all the outside world are blurred, out of focus.

But even though this death is a wall that you cannot climb over or burrow under, that stretches so far, too far to find a way around it, you needn't go crashing into it again and again and again. You can instead seek to take in all there is before the wall, before the wall and beyond the death. The ache, the knowledge that you've been so cruelly cheated, will, I suppose, be with you as long as you live. But the fact that your mother died while you were still an infant is not the most important nor the most interesting thing about you.

What is there before the wall and beyond the death? There is love, and there is life, and, as you have surely learned by now, there is even laughter. And there is opportunity: This is, still, a badly fractured planet, and there are those who devote themselves to mending its fractures. There is nobility and there is vulgarity, and therefore there is room for you to take a stand. "I have put before you life and death," the Bible teaches; "blessing and curse; now choose life."

I move, as you will long since have come to know, back and forth from the deeply personal to the crashingly political, from the private to the public. I make no excuses for that, even though I sometimes wish I were better at balancing the two. But the private stuff is too often elusive.

The harsh truth of the matter is that one need not experience disarray directly, as our family has, in order to be fully aware of it. Turn on the television news, read the newspapers, go through life with open eyes, and not a day, scarcely an hour, will pass without reconfirmation of how very far we remain from the world the poets and the prophets describe: the world of justice and of loving-kindness.

You will, I expect, because of the stock you come from, because of your father and the family and friends who've raised you, and perhaps because of your own wound, too, be tormented by the world's distress and therefore make room for it in your own life. Yet there will likely be times when all the hurt and all the pain overwhelm, become too much to bear.

I know. There's a line in our Grace After Meals that I (as also many others) am unable to bring myself to sing: "I was young, and I have grown old, and I have never seen the righteous so forsaken that his seed must beg bread." There are interpretations of that passage that try to work around its obvious contradiction of everything we see and know. But none I have heard satisfies me, so distant is the statement from my experience. Bad things do happen to good people, and good things to bad, and there are times when the whole enterprise seems very nearly random.

I don't know how to say this next without sounding like old Polonius, so forgive me if by the time you read the words they are so obvious to you as to border on (or cross over into) the banal: There is one thing of which we may be absolutely certain: If we react to the apparent randomness by scoffing at goodness, by withholding our kindness—after all, what purpose do these serve if all there is, is accident?—we add to the world's chaos. And it's true: There is no guarantee that our effort for good will change anything, will have any enduring impact. But the absence of a guarantee is not an argument. On the other side, our refusal to enlist in the ranks of the world-menders, whether in large ways or in small, ensures that the world will go unmended.

I know no way around these venerable ideas, clichés though they may long since have become. I accept that the notion that "from those to whom much has been given, much is required" has grown tiresome. But I so want you to know that much, very much, has been given you. As against the rude loss you've suffered, there's the great love you've known, and the rich freedom that is yours as an American, and the great wisdom and the abiding hope that are yours as a Jew, and the compassion and the concern for justice that are yours because of the family into which you were born. These gifts are yours—so long as you make use of them. They come not as offsets to the loss; the loss is there, now and always. But so are these other things, if you so will it.

A friend with whom I've talked about these things asks bluntly, as is her useful way: If you mean it when you say that every moment of every day, the spinning wheel stops somewhere that it is not supposed to, somewhere that makes no sense; that every moment of every day, somewhere, a parent is bereaved, a child is untimely orphaned, a dream dissolves; that *this* time, the wheel stopped here—then how can you mean what you say when you refer to the Jews, or even just to your own family, as "prisoners of hope," or when you cite approvingly Nomi's letter to the Natansohns and its assertion of trust and faith?

Indeed. But the hope I assert is an act of defiance. Even on those days—there are many—when the evidence sneers at the hope, there are friends and colleagues to help sustain it, as also memories of other and better days. And the faith is born of my conviction that so much of the pain and even the death is avoidable. Yes, there will always be babies born who are doomed to die young. But surely death from hunger is not a phenomenon to which we must fatalistically resign ourselves. Nor maiming or death from stepping on a leftover land mine. Nor so much of the insult and injury that wounds so many people.

On your mother's thirtieth birthday—her last—we went to Tanglewood, summer home of the Boston Symphony. ("We" means Nomi and David, Rachel, Jessie and Rob, Sharon and I.) The timing could not have been better, at least from my standpoint, since the program for that evening was the Verdi Requiem, which is not only among my very favorite pieces of music but which includes as well my most favorite musical moment. No recording can compare to a live performance, and this was an opportunity not only to share my beloved music with my beloved family, but perhaps as well to induct a new generation into an endangered musical taste.

The Verdi: It's a long piece and more operatic than the typical requiem. Very near its end, in the *Libera Me*, the entire orchestra and chorus are going full-blast when suddenly, the voice of the soprano soloist comes soaring over them all. That moment, which I've by now heard hundreds of times, never fails to induce in me a physical response.

The reason for that response may be entirely visceral, something to do with the ways in which music can and sometimes does reach deep, deep inside us. But about this particular musical moment I have a rather different theory. Above the fireplace in my living room there hangs a drawing (more accurately, a copy of a drawing) by Kathe Kollwitz. It is part of her "Peasant's War" series of 1903, and it depicts a horde of barely human figures, people who have quite obviously been beaten down, brutalized, now all on the move, surging forward, urged on by a figure we see only from the rear. Her raised arms give the drawing its direction, and the mass of people theirs. She has roused them, she encourages them, they can yet be free.

And where does Verdi's soprano fit?

Here is what one person can do: One person can break through almost any barrier, can break out of a massed orchestra and chorus or years of oppression and be heard. And the hands and the voice can heal, can mend.

So yes, eyes open to a world too often cruel, so often random in its verdicts—and hope, and faith, for without these, what is left? Take the exchange of letters between your mother and Sam Natansohn to heart; it is yours by right.

How I wish it could end there, a comforting moral to heal the wounded heart. Become a mender, and all will be mended—the heart, too. But you know that there are wounds that can never heal, fractures that cannot be mended, fractures that are—here's that terrifying word again—forever.

Do your mother's words, or Sam Natansohn's words, or mine, then come merely as a verbal veneer, pasted atop the void we know to be the fundamental truth? No. There is no single truth. Sorrow is a truth, but no more than hope; loss is a truth, but no more than love. The words we use to help relieve the pain of all the slings and all the arrows are also, used wisely, more than a relief; they are a defense against outrageous fortune. They encourage us to struggle against the despair of defeat, even of death. And although rude fate will intervene to mock our struggle, we will not concede.

Liat: I wrote much earlier in these pages that no life is entirely a new beginning. Some of what we know we know because others have learned it and found a way to teach it to us. Words are one such way. They serve as signposts, and though you may take unmarked roads, you are entitled to know the paths that others who love you commend to you. Whatever the paths you choose, whether they are wholly untraveled or long since cleared by others, you will make them your own. For even though many others may have walked a particular path, each time you follow its bend will be for you the first. I cannot describe for you the fragrance of a rose; I can only tell you that this way, you will encounter a rose, and that I and others have found pleasure in that. And , there, a thorn: Take care.

Here is some of what others have learned—and taught: Your mother's maternal grandfather, Yoine, was a paper-hanger, and her maternal grandmother, Tamara, a pieceworker in a garment factory. Once each week, Tamara would count the tags from the items she had that week basted, and her pay for that week was based on the total number of items. Not infrequently, the basting needle would slip and penetrate her finger. When that happened, she'd go to the clinic built and maintained by the Amalgamated Clothing Workers of America, a trade union that sustained her sense of dignity as her employer did not.

Yoine and Tamar were humble people, displaced by history, immigrants to this country and devoted, as so many of the immigrant generation were, to making a better life for their children—in their case, for your grandmother, their only child.

I didn't know Yoine well. He was a small man, and quiet, with thick-lensed eyeglasses, and I was unable to tie anything I knew of him to the photograph from the old country, Yoineh as a young and handsome man who had been an ice-skating champion and a powerful swimmer, who played a variety of musical instruments and spoke six languages. By the time I knew him, he had retreated into himself, and all the stories of his early years were of so different a time they might as well have been of a different person.

But I've known your great-grandmother Tamara, who is now in her mid-nineties, for many years. She is a rare woman. One can still see in her wrinkled face the sparkling-eyed beauty she was, and if one talks with her for any length of time, one still finds in her a person of lively interests and intelligence. I've often wondered what might have been had she lived a more ordered life and been educated properly. But she did not, was not. Her life was instead definitively shaped by the experience of immigration, which is also, by definition, an experience of emigration, the trauma of leaving behind everything one has known, followed by the trauma of arriving to a place and a people unknown. She rarely relaxed; mostly, she vacillated between nervousness and fear.

Still, talk to her even now of world events and she readily carries her end of the conversation; during the years I knew her best, she daily read a Yiddish paper, she cared deeply about the larger world. And the smaller world, too: Though poor—she and Yoine had a one-bedroom apartment, their daughter (your grandmother) sleeping on the living room couch—she would regularly set aside enough money to send food and clothing to her half-sisters in Russia.

By and large, that generation of immigrants—my parents and your grandmothers' parents, your father's grandparents, too—accomplished what they had set out to accomplish: They gave to their children lives far, far richer in promise than the Old Country would have offered. One sees the effort still, in the case of the Russian Jews, many of them college-educated professionals, who've lately come to America, who take the most menial jobs when only such jobs are available, but are determined to hand on to their children America's golden promise. And among the Vietnamese and the Mexicans and very, very many of the groups that have made up the contemporary immigration to these shores. It is well to bear in mind their devotion. It is a worthy example to us all.

Yoine, for his part, spent many of his days—by the time I knew him, he was working only sporadically—playing chess or pinochle with his handful of friends. (Chess, weather permitting, in the park; pinochle in the back room of the neighborhood barbershop or delicatessen.) It was our habit to call Yoine and Tamara pretty much every day, and when I'd make the call and Yoine would answer, I'd always begin by asking how he was. The invariable answer: "A little better." A little better every day, until the day before, mercifully, he died in his sleep.

When we came back from the cemetery after his burial, we were lacking the required ten men for the *minyan*. (Back then, it would not have occurred to any of us to count women. Today, of course, it would not occur to us to omit them.) Knowing that the candy store across the street was owned by a Jew, I went to the store and, although its owner didn't know me, I informed him that we were sitting *shiva*—mourning—across the street and that we lacked a tenth person for our prayers. Without hesitation, he asked me to wait a moment while he locked the store, and he came with me.

I've never forgotten that tiny episode. From it, I derive the importance of community, at times of a faceless community, where people still feel connected by a culture of reciprocal responsibilities. But I derive, as well, the importance of being ready, at any moment of any day, to be the tenth person in a *minyan,* to be the person who makes the difference in transforming an aggregation of people into a purposeful cohort.

And, by (substantial) extension, the importance of being prepared, when occasion warrants, to be the first person in a *minyan*, to take a position and stand your ground until others begin to congregate around you, thereby enabling actions that would otherwise be impossible to undertake. Verdi's Requiem and Kollwitz's drawing again, the power of one.

Just before she died, your mother arranged for a professional video interview of Tamara, who was then approaching ninety. Nomi intended that video for you. (As you watch it, you'll notice that now and then Tamara glances off to the side, away from the camera; that's when she's turning to Nomi, who is standing just off-camera.) By the time you watch it, you may well have heard endless Tamara stories. Set those aside, if you can, and watch and listen to the story of a woman whose life spans nearly the whole of this century, a woman—your own great-grandmother—who lived through the Russian revolution, who followed the much-traveled path to a new life in North America, whose "new life" was one of hard, hard work and near poverty—and who retained her dignity, her curiosity, and her generosity through it all. You will know her, if at all, only as a very old woman. All of us are in debt to your mother for arranging an interview that comes to remind us of the life that came before.

Stories, and then more stories. Lives, really, for in the end, the stories are what remain of the lives. But I do not mean this as a collection of all your mother's family's stories, those your mother would have told you as also some she herself never knew. (Although I do feel the press of time: Who knows which of us of the older generation, your grandparents, my brother, others a half-century and more older than you, will be here to tell you these stories by the time you are able to absorb them? And your father's stories you will have to ask him to gather for you.) Bear with me: These are your inheritance, the stuff that can never be cloned.

My father and mother, your great-grandparents, were teachers. They, too, were immigrants; they'd eloped and soon after came to this country, to Ellis Island. Over the course of many years, they lived in New York and in Atlanta, in Detroit and in Pittsburgh, in Winnipeg and Bridgeport and finally in Baltimore, where I did most of my growing up.

When my father retired after many years of teaching at the Baltimore Hebrew College, he was tendered a farewell dinner. After all the speeches honoring him as a teacher, it was his turn to respond:

> When I was a boy, the rebbe in our *heder* [school] in Binder [a city in Bessarabia, now Moldavia] said to us one day, "Children, they say that very far away, there is a country called America, and I suppose that is so, for why would they lie about such a thing? And they say as well that in that far-away country called America, there is a city called Philadelphia, and I suppose that, too, is so. And they go on to say that in the city called Philadelphia, there is a bell they call the Liberty Bell, and that on that bell are proclaimed words from our book: 'Proclaim liberty throughout the land and to all the inhabitants thereof.' Frankly, I find that hard to believe. Why would they write our words on their bell?
>
> "I have a favor to ask of you now. If it should happen when you grow up that you go to America, try to visit the place they call Philadelphia and see the bell. And write and tell me whether it is true that they have

inscribed our words on their bell. I would like to know such a thing."

And my father continued,

As it happened, I did come to America, and I chanced to Philadelphia, and I went to see the bell, and yes, indeed, there were the words, our words. But the bell was cracked.

You honor me tonight for my life as a teacher. I prefer to think of myself as a person who has tried to live his life as a bell-mender.

That's the tradition into which Rachel and Jessie and your mother were born and in which they were raised. When the kids in your mother's class at Schechter were ready to begin their study of Bible, my father—by then a very grandfatherly looking man—was invited to get them started by telling them of his first day, back in a city we knew as Binder, in a place now known as Moldava. He charmed them utterly, and for years thereafter he served as the institutional grandfather, bridging the storied past and the new adventure upon which the third-graders were deemed old enough to embark. In time, the students' parents would "happen" to be in the school on the day he was to speak, and they'd line the walls of the classroom where their children sat in a circle and listened to the old man. And your mother was so very proud of him. And he, of course, of her.

"The bell" is, of course, a metaphor for the larger mending that awaits, the mending of a world disordered. *Tikkun olam*, that's called in Hebrew, and your mother knew that it was her destiny, one way or another, to join the company of menders. She knew that and embraced it. Paying attention to her friends, chatting with a schizophrenic man on a park bench, thinking carefully about the mass media in our society, and in a dozen other ways, a healer, a fixer, a mender. And above all, of course, a mom, *your* mom, pouring all her intelligence and her enthusiasm and her love into getting you started, into you.

Liat, Liat: These last words I write as I sit in the Martha's Vineyard home of my dear friend and colleague Rachel Cowan. The house is empty. Behind the computer on which I'm typing are three windows. Through them I see the waters of Menemsha Creek and, across the way, the hills that lead to Gay's Head. Just a handful of houses are visible; otherwise, the scene is timeless. Birds soar and swoop and startle. The sky is gray, the weather unseasonably cold.

And I think of my daughter, and of you, her daughter, whom I want so much to comfort. I want for you, my love, flesh of my flesh and bone of my bone, that you will be whole. The emptiness cannot be wished away, nor is there reason to try. All we need guard against is the swelling of the emptiness, its displacement of the other truths of our lives. You are the daughter of a mother who died just 500 days after you were born. But for sure her story did not end in January of 1996. Her death is a sorry fact of your life—but not, I pray, the defining fact. There is much, much more to her story than the tragedy of her death—and all that is yours, too. For my own sake and for yours, I wish for you—as Jessie once put it—that there will be much Nominess in you: the grace, the elegance of mind and the loveliness of spirit, the rich capacity for love and friendship, the heightened sense of empathy, the eagerness to celebrate and the readiness to mourn.

More even than that, I wish for you to be Liat, your own person, a compassionate child of a compassionate mother, of a compassionate family and tradition, worthy and willing heir to all that implies, link in such ways as suit you in a chain that is not broken.

Liat, more even than you and your father and the rest of us, your mother was miserably cheated. She didn't get to see how the story unfolds, much less how it ends. But she knew, better than most, the underlying truth: The story never ends. All that changes is who gets to write it. It's your turn now; write honestly and well.